…OT · AMERIGO VESPUCCI, GIOVANNI DA VERRAZZANO…
…E TONTY · FILIPPO MAZZEI · FRANCESCO V…
… RODNEY · CAESAR AUGUSTUS RODNEY…GIUSEPPE GAR…
…CCHIO · ERCOLE SALVETTI · AMBROGIO SCOPINI · OLIV…
…ESNOLA · ENRICO FARDELLA V. EDUARDO FERRERO ·…
…ACOB PHINIZI · FRANK ARRIGHI · KING VITTORIO EMAN…
…AGUARDIA · JOHN BASILONE · DON GENTILE · GIUSEPP…
…RESCA . SALVATORE NINFO · MARIA AND PIETRO BOTT…
…TEVE GEPPI · ANTONIO PASIN . ROBERT DI ROMUALDO…
…USEPPE SIMI · GIOVANNI FOPPIANO · VITTORIO SATTUI…
…AND MATT GALLO · ROBERT MONDAVI · CESARE AND R…
…TTORE BOIARDI · AMEDEO OBICI · MARIO PERUZZI · VI…
…ARRO · DOMENICO GHIRARDELLI · ANTHONY ROSSI · TA…
…UPO · ROGER ENRICO · AMADEO P. GIANNINI · GEORGE…
… BARSOTTI · GIUSEPPE CECCHI · PETER F. SECCHIA · LEA…
… JACUZZI FAMILY · BERNARD (BEN) CAMMARATA . STEVE…
…II · LEONARD S. RIGGIO · WILLIAM CAFARO · EDWARD…
…CESO GAZZOLO · LEE IACOCCA · JOHN RICCARDO · EUG…
…UCIO A. NOTO · VINCENT J. TROSINO · ALFRED A. CHE…
… SALVATORE F. SODANO · CARL PASCARELLA · ANGELO…
…MAS MARSICO · PATRICIA RUSSO · PAMELA FIORI · GRACE…
… · ONOFRIO RAZZOLINI · JOHN PHINIZY · ANTHONY G…
…ROSINO · CHARLIE ANGELO SIRINGO · FRANCIS B. SPINO…
…LFRED E. SMITH · VINCENT PALMISANO · PETER CAVIC…
…OSI · VITO MARCANTONIO · CHARLES MARGIOTTI · ANG…
…NCATO · MICHAEL A. MUSMANNO · PETER RODINO · JO…
…EZZE · EDWARD CORSI · VINCENT IMPELLITTERI · GIUS…
…RIZZO . RICHARD CALIGIURI · ELLA TAMBUSSI GRASSO…
…TI · JOSEPH CALIFANO · FRANK C. CARLUCCI · JOHN A. …
…NE · MARIO CUOMO · GEORGE E. PATAKI · RUDOLPH W…
…E DOMINICI · ALPHONSE D'AMATO · ANTONIN SCALIA…

ITALIANS IN AMERICA

ITALI

ITALIANS IN AMERICA
A Celebration

CATALDO LEONE

with Contributions by Dona De Sanctis,
Ron Onesti and Tim Preston

A MOCKINGBIRD BOOK,
PUBLISHED WITH PORTFOLIO PRESS

FOR THE NATIONAL
ITALIAN AMERICAN
FOUNDATION

Copyright © 2001 by Mockingbird Press and Portfolio Press

All rights reserved.

No part of this book may be reproduced by any means without written permission of the publisher.

Printed in Italy by Milanostampa, S.p.A.

First Edition

PICTURE CREDITS

Abbreviations:
National Italian American Foundation = NIAF
Library of Congress = LC
National Italian American Sports Hall of Fame, Chicago = NIASHF

Half-title: Corbis; ix: NIAF; x: Leon Panetta; xvi: LC; 3(top and bottom): NIAF; 5 (top): LC; 5 (bottom): NIAF; 6: LC; 7: LC; 8: LC; 10: LC; 12 (top and bottom): NIAF; 15: NIAF; 16: LC; 18: LC; 19: LC; 20 (top and bottom): LC; 22 (top and bottom): LC; 23: LC; 24: LC; 25: LC; 26-27: LC; 28: NIAF; 31: Frank Fede; 32: LC; 34: LC; 35: LC; 36: LC; 39 (top and bottom): LC; 40: LC; 43: LC; 45 (top and bottom): LC; 46: Ferrara Bakery; 49: Castello Banfi; 50-51: Robert Mondavi Winery; 53: A. Pastan; 54-55: Stockphoto; 58 (left and right): NIAF; 62: Peter Secchia, Ben Cammarata, Andy Giancomelli, Roger Enrico; 63: Lee Iacocca; 64: J. Terrence Lanni; 65: Michael Renzulli; 66: Robert Di Romualdo, Livio DeSimone, Leonard Riggio; 66-67 (background): Stockphoto; 67 (left): Office of Mayor Rudolph Giuliani; 67 (right): John F. Antioco; 68 Pamela Fiori; 69: John Paul DeJoria; 70: NIAF; 71: NIAF; 72 (left): George Graziadio; 72 (right): Ronald Zarrella ; 73: Vincent Trosino; 74 (top): NIAF; 74 (bottom): Stephen J. Belmonte; 75 (top):Robert Georgine; 75 (bottom): Lawrence Auriana; 76 (top): Jerry Colangelo; 76 (bottom, left): NIAF; 76 (bottom, right): Carmen Policy; 78: LC; 80: LC; 83: LC; 85: LC; 86: Corbis; 89 (top and bottom): NIAF; 90-91: National Portrait Gallery, Smithsonian Institution; 92-93 (top and bottom): NIAF; 92-93 (background): LC; 94 (top and bottom): NIAF; 94 (background): Corbis; 96: NIAF; 98: National Portrait Gallery, Smithsonian Institution; 101: LC; 102 (top and bottom): LC; 103: NIAF; 105: NIAF; 106: LC; 107: LC; 109: LC; 111(top left and right): LC; 111 (bottom left): NIAF; 112: NIAF; 114 (top left and right): NIAF; 114 (bottom left): National Portrait Gallery, Smithsonian Institution; 115 (top and bottom): NIAF; 119 (left): LC; 119 (right): NIAF; 120 (left and right): NIAF; 122: NIAF; 123: LC; 124: NIAF; 126: NIAF; 128: NIASHF; 134: NIASHF; 136 (top): NIASHF; 136 (bottom): LC; 136 (background): Stockphoto; 137: NIASHF; 139: NIAF; 140: NIASHF; 143: NIASHF; 143 (background): Stockphoto; 149: NIASHF; 152 (top, center, bottom): NIASHF; 152 (background): Corbis; 153: NIASHF; 154: NIASHF; 155: NIASHF; 156: NIASHF; 157: NIASHF; 158: NIASHF; 159: LC; 160: NIASHF; 163: NIASHF; 164: LC; 167: LC; 168: LC; 169: LC; 170 (left and right): NIAF; 172: LC; 173: NIAF; 175: NIAF; 177: NIAF; 178: The Granger Collection, New York; 181: LC; 184: LC; 186: Corbis; 189: NIAF; 190: Corbis; 192 (top and bottom): NIAF; 193: NIAF; 194: NIAF; 195: NIAF; 197: Corbis; 201: Corbis; 202: Maria Bartiromo.

CONTENTS

vii PUBLISHER'S NOTE

ix PREFACE

xii FOREWORD

xiv ACKNOWLEDGMENTS

1 ITALIAN AMERICANS IN U.S. HISTORY

17 PURSUING THE DREAM

33 SUFFERING AND SACRIFICE

47 BUSINESS AND ENTREPRENEURS

79 A STRONG VOICE

99 ARTS AND ENTERTAINMENT

129 SPORTS

165 EDUCATION, SCIENCE AND MEDICINE

179 ITALIAN-AMERICAN WOMEN

199 ITALIAN AMERICANS IN THE MAINSTREAM

205 AFTERWORD

PUBLISHER'S NOTE

I came to the United States forty years ago on a student visa to attend the Art Students League in New York City. When I arrived, the first thing I learned was that Italians were stereotyped either as "Latin lovers" or as gangsters—sometimes as both. I was surprised to discover that all the young men and women of Italian descent I met knew nothing of Italy and its history and, even more disturbingly, did not care. They were all proud to be American but not very proud to be Italian, having felt the brunt of negative stereotyping.

With *Italians in America: A Celebration*, we are attempting to show our readers why Americans of Italian descent have good reason to be proud to be both Italians and Americans, to be proud of their Italian culture as well as of the great contribution Italian Americans have made to this country, and why we should all celebrate what we have accomplished. This book tells the story of where we came from, where we are now, and where we are going. We feel the sky is the limit for Italians in America.

SANDRO DIANI

Mockingbird Books

PREFACE

Frank J. Guarini represented New Jersey in the U.S. Congress before becoming chairman of the National Italian American Foundation.

We Italian Americans know the stories of our families' early experiences in this country. How *nonno* came over as a boy with only twenty-five dollars in his pocket and had to sleep in the park his first three days in America until he found work in the mines. How *nonna* was sick the entire two weeks of the ocean voyage and saw snow for the first time when she came to America.

We know how hard our parents and grandparents worked and saved to buy a house or start a business so they could earn their way out of poverty and up the ladder of success in this land of endless possibilities and countless opportunities. And we are justly proud that, in only three or four generations, our families have achieved great personal and professional success.

But what we don't know is the history of Italian Americans as a people in this country. We don't know that Italian Americans are one of this country's greatest success stories. Our accomplishments in this land are living proof that America keeps its promise to "the huddled masses."

As a result of the great freedom, opportunity, and social mobility we found here, Italian Americans have been able to make remarkable contributions. We have established such huge businesses and corporations as Barnes & Noble, Planters Peanuts, Tropicana Orange Juice, and the Bank of America, to name only a few. We also decorated the Capitol dome, sculpted the Lincoln Memorial, discovered the virus that causes leukemia, and developed the shopping mall.

But our history in this country goes much further back than the last century. Italians have played a role in the United States since its very beginnings. In fact, two men of Italian descent signed the Declaration of Independence: William Paca of Maryland and Caesar Rodney of Delaware, both of whom later became governors of their respective states. Three regiments totaling fifteen hundred Italian soldiers helped fight the British in the American Revolution.

In the Civil War, thousands of Italian Americans fought in both the Union and Confederate armies, including four generals and more than one hundred officers in the Union Army. Italian Americans were among the first to volunteer to serve in both world wars, as well as in Korea and Vietnam. At least thirty-nine Italian Americans are U.S. Congressional Medal of Honor recipients, the first dating from the Civil War.

Italian Americans have been governors, senators, members of Congress, and mayors, as well as inventors of many useful modern conveniences such as the Jacuzzi, the coffeemaker, the tape deck, and the three-way light bulb.

This long history of achievement is even more impressive when we consider the equally long history of persecution our immigrant forebears endured here. Italian immigrants were lynched in the South, paid less than white and black Americans in the North, forced to worship in the basements of churches, and encouraged to change their names, deny their heritage, and teach their children English instead of Italian. Only sixty years ago, during World War II, Italian Americans were subjected to curfews, confiscation of property, and in some cases even internment.

Our children do not learn these facts in school because they are not in the textbooks. Instead of hearing about the factual history of Italians in America, our children, along with the rest of the country, learn about Italian Americans through the fictionalized portrayal of us as criminals, racists, and born losers on television and in the movies. We owe this untrue depiction to the U.S. entertainment industry, but part of it is our fault, as well.

How many books on Italian-American history do we have in our home libraries? How many of us encourage our children to study Italian? How many of us dismiss as "only make-believe" the movies, television programs, and commercials that stereotype us?

The book you are holding in your hands is an effort by the National Italian

American Foundation to correct this situation by informing Italian Americans about their proud past. Here you will find historic photographs and carefully researched chapters about Italian Americans in U.S. history. Here you will learn about the explorers, military leaders, scientists, financial wizards, educators, and athletes who excelled—and by excelling made enormous contributions to American life.

The National Italian American Foundation undertook this project because it believes in the vital importance of turning all Italian Americans into ambassadors of their heritage. To do so we first must educate ourselves about Italian-American history and culture, and then must teach what we have learned to our children, family, friends, and community.

Yes, it is important to know your family's history in America, but it is just as important to know the rest of the story. *Italians in America: A Celebration* aims to tell this remarkable story. We urge you to read it carefully and then share it with your family and friends.

FRANK J. GUARINI, Chairman
National Italian American Foundation

FOREWORD

Leon Panetta is the son of Calabrian immigrants who settled in California. He is a former U.S. Congressman, and the first Italian American ever to serve as White House Chief of Staff.

Italy has contributed more to the world than any nation in history. One way to understand the importance of these contributions would be to see what would be left if we took everything Italian from the world. What a loss for music, art, engineering, design, literature, and life's little luxuries—good food, fine wine, and high fashion. And what a loss for the United States, which would no longer have an estimated twenty million Americans of Italian descent, the children and grandchildren of the Italian immigrants who came to this country more than a century ago.

The history and contributions of these Italian Americans are captured in *Italians in America: A Celebration*. On these pages you will find ample evidence of the sizable but little-known accomplishments of Italian Americans in science, medicine, law enforcement, business, education, and many other fields.

This book also reaches beyond the nineteenth-century immigrant experience to highlight the role Italians played in the American Revolution, the Civil War, the labor movement, national and local politics, and the arts, as well as sports, entertainment, and popular music. These achievements are even more significant when one considers the long and painful history that shaped the character of the early Italian immigrants who came to America so long ago.

In 1870 Italy's long struggle to be unified ended when Italian troops stormed Rome, wresting it from the Vatican and making it the capital of the newly formed country of Italy. Unification was a mixed blessing, especially for the poor and powerless farmers and peasants in the south. Their taxes rose and their sons were drafted into the new Italian army.

In Southern Italy at that time, thirteen thousand families of the aristocracy and middle class owned eleven million acres, leaving barely one million acres for the 2.3 million peasants who owned land. One of every four peasants, however, did not own any property. They considered themselves fortunate if they found work six months out of the year, because the great landowners were not interested in farming, and productivity suffered accordingly.

A growing tide of Italians, most of them from Southern Italy, began emigrating to the United States and South America, where work was plentiful and land was cheap. The exodus of southern Italians from their villages at the turn of the twentieth century has no parallel in history. Out of a total population of fourteen million in Southern Italy at the time of national unification, at least five million—more than one third of the population—left to work overseas by the outbreak of World War I. In all of Italy, more than eleven million people—a quarter of the population—emigrated between 1881 and 1911.

More than four million Italians came to the United States during what we now call the Great Migration, the forty-two-year period between 1880 and 1922. About three million of these immigrants became permanent residents and many also became American citizens—including my parents, Carmelo and Carmelina Panetta from Calabria. In 1922 the United States passed federal laws that restricted immigration of Southern and Eastern Europeans—largely Italians and Jews—to this country, and immigration dwindled markedly.

Those Italian Americans whose parents and grandparents came to the United States during the Great Migration have firsthand knowledge of that massive exodus. Today they number an estimated twenty million—the nation's fifth-largest ethnic group after the Germans, Irish, English, and African Americans, according to the U.S. Census Bureau.

Fully assimilated into American society, they are leaders in business, the professions, and government. Antonin Scalia, the son of Sicilian immigrants, sits on the U. S. Supreme Court; Leonard Riggio heads Barnes & Noble; Catherine De Angelis is editor of the *Journal of the American Medical Association;* Richard Grasso chairs the New York Stock Exchange; Penny Marshall (née Masciarelli) is one of the most successful directors in Hollywood; and thirty-one men and women of Italian descent, including five senators and four Congresswomen, were serving in Congress as the twentieth century drew to a close.

The story of their success honors them and the United States, a nation that gave millions of largely poor and unschooled Italian peasants limitless opportunities. Social scientists have yet to analyze the elements of Italian working-class culture that enabled so many millions of immigrants to achieve success abroad despite language barriers, new schools, often unfair and unfavorable economic and employment practices, and the prejudices, suspicions, and hostility of their new neighbors, long established on these shores.

Despite these obstacles, the Italian immigrants and their children triumphed in America. The dramatic story of their struggles and successes has been captured on these pages so that future generations can learn of this truly remarkable chapter in our history.

LEON PANETTA

The Leon & Sylvia Panetta Institute for Public Policy

ACKNOWLEDGMENTS

The National Italian American Foundation (NIAF) wishes to acknowledge the efforts of the following individuals who assisted with the publication of this book:

Sandro Diani, publisher, Mockingbird Press; Robert Rowe, president, Portfolio Press; Cataldo Leone, primary author of the volume; Dona De Sanctis, NIAF's director of Research and Cultural Affairs, as well as editor-in-chief of the book and author of the chapter on women; Gay Talese, volume editor; Leon Panetta, author of the Foreword; Maria Bartiromo, author of the Afterword; Frank Guarini, NIAF chairman; John Salmone, NIAF's director of Special Projects; Geraldine Jones-Roche, NIAF's deputy director, Special Projects; Ron Onesti and Tim Preston, authors of the sports chapter; Carole McCurdy, copy editor; Linda McKnight, designer, and Amy Pastan, managing editor. We would also like to express our gratitude to the Library of Congress photoduplication office and to George Randazzo of the National Italian American Sports Hall of Fame, for generously providing us with images from their collections.

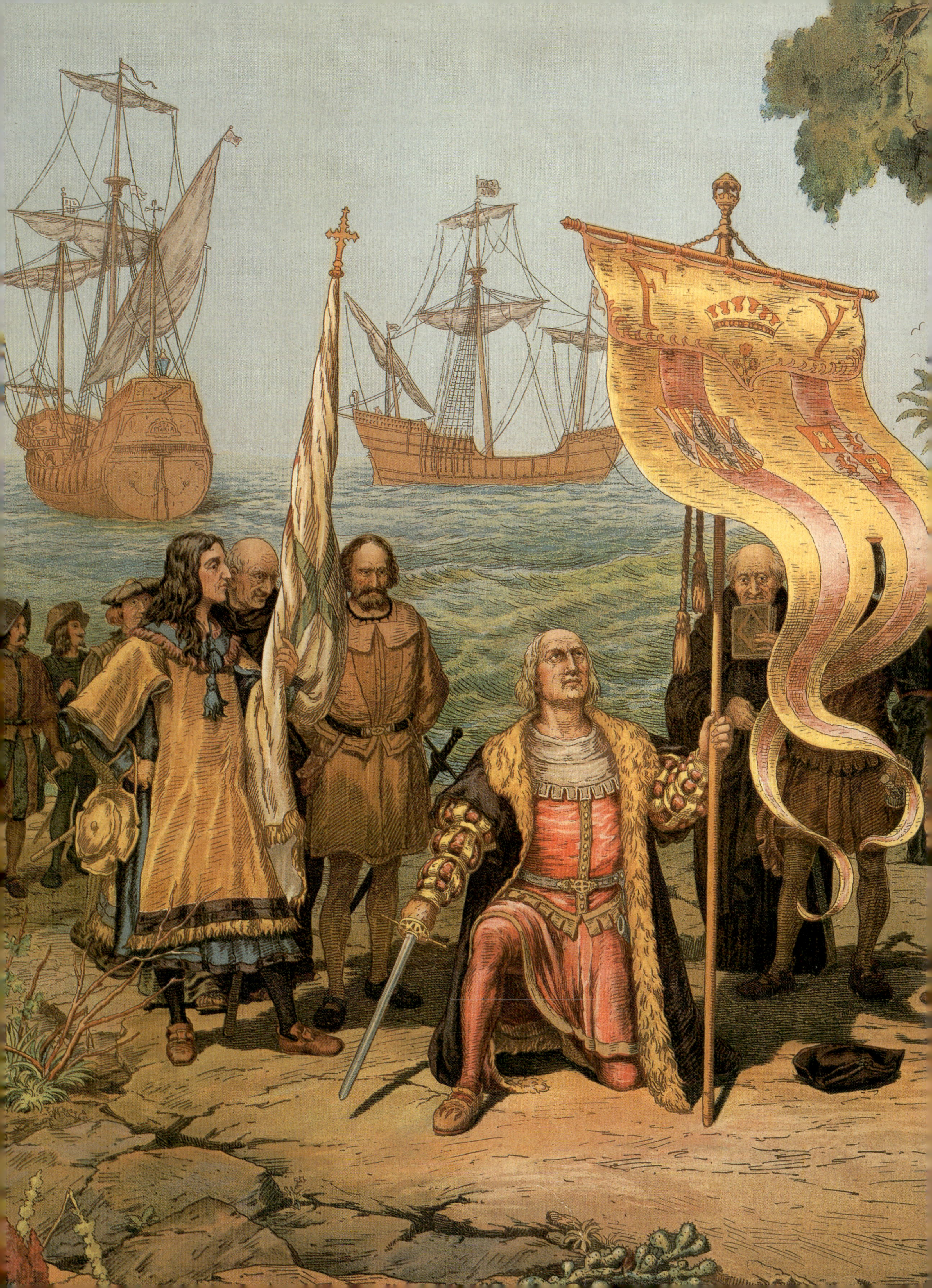
F
Y

ITALIAN AMERICANS IN U.S. HISTORY

Italians have played an important part in every stage of American history, from the discovery of the New World to its colonization, from independence to the Civil War, and from the two world wars to the present.

Many of the early explorers and navigators who charted courses through unknown and dangerous waters to America were Italian. In both history and legend, the most famous of all was Christopher Columbus.

THE AGE OF EXPLORATION

Christopher Columbus (Cristoforo Colombo) was a Genoese who set out in search of Asia with three ships flying Spanish colors. After little more than three weeks at sea, Columbus and his crew sighted land on October 12, 1492. What they believed to be the Indies was in truth an island in the Caribbean, but even after three more voyages the great Italian explorer remained firm in his conviction that the land he had reached was Asia.

Nevertheless, the fact remains that the geography of the world was forever changed thanks to an Italian, a fact remembered every year in the United States on Columbus Day. The first celebration of Columbus Day came soon after the American Revolution: on October 12, 1792, the New York Society of Tammany honored Columbus on the three hundredth anniversary of his first voyage. In 1920, October 12 became a legal holiday in more

This image of Columbus's landing in America hangs in the U.S. Capitol. It was painted by John Van der Lyn, an early American artist (1776–1852).

than thirty states but it wasn't until 1973 that it became a federal holiday in all fifty states.

At the same time, John Cabot (Giovanni Caboto)—another experienced and ambitious navigator who, like Columbus, was born in Genoa—aspired to find a sea route to the East Indies. Cabot imagined that a faster and easier route to the East Indies could be found by setting sail from a point further north than Columbus had. King Henry VII of England agreed to authorize the expedition, and in 1497 Cabot set sail from Bristol with a crew of eighteen, several of whom were Italian.

When he came ashore on the coast of what is now Newfoundland, he believed he had reached the northeastern shores of Asia. The following year Henry VII, satisfied with the results of the expedition, offered to finance another voyage, destined to be Cabot's last. The explorer died at sea before he was able to gather further knowledge regarding the mysterious land he had found, but his efforts were not in vain. His son, Sebastian Cabot, who had accompanied him on his two voyages, put his inheritance of knowledge to good use. He became a skilled navigator and returned to the new continent, flying first the English flag and later the banner of Spain. The Cabots' experiences contributed greatly to broadening the world's horizons. Only in their wake were other navigators able to add more pieces to the puzzle that would in time reveal the face of America.

The very name "America" is a tribute to Italy. It was introduced into the language in honor of the Florentine explorer and geographer Amerigo Vespucci, who sailed to the New World (specifically, to Brazil) in 1499. He was the first to believe that this new land was not the Indies but a hitherto unknown continent.

The first expedition to explore the North American coast was led by another Florentine navigator, Giovanni da Verrazzano, sent by King Frances I of France to find a sea route to China. Verrazzano reached the coast of North Carolina at the point known today as Cape Fear, then sailed up the coast and into New York Bay in 1524, arriving there eighty years before the Dutchman Henry Hudson. Today the bridge that links Brooklyn to Staten Island, one of the longest in the world, bears his name.

Right, above: Columbus, born in Genoa in 1451, claimed possession of the New World for Spain. He actually made four trips to the New World. He died in 1506.

Right, below: Two intrepid explorers of Italian heritage were John Cabot (Giovanni Caboto) and his son Sebastian. Sponsored by Britain, John Cabot's discovery in 1497 of what is now Newfoundland led to the English colonization in North America.

HISTORY
3

ITALIANS IN COLONIAL AMERICA

Thanks in part to these Italian explorers, the contours of America were becoming clearer. In the meantime, a small but constant stream of Italians began arriving on its shores. As early as 1610, Italian master glassblowers had taken up residence in Jamestown, Virginia—the first English settlement in the New World. But the first relatively large immigration of Italians occurred in 1657, when a group of three hundred Piedmontese Protestants landed in New York. Their journey ended in Delaware, where they established the first government of the colony of New Amstel, now called New Castle.

At the beginning of the eighteenth century, the Italian population in America numbered a few thousand, but that figure was destined to rise. Among the Italian colonists were young, talented craftsmen and skilled merchants. Others were missionaries sent by the Spanish or the English with the aim of establishing peaceful relations with the Native Americans, to strengthen these European powers' hold on the territories as yet unexplored.

One of these missionaries was the Jesuit Eusebio Francesco Chino. His formidable qualities as a teacher, cosmographer, explorer, and man of faith enabled him to expand the Spanish possessions from the Colorado River to the Gulf of Mexico.

One of the first examples of Italian entrepreneurship in the New World was provided by the fur trader Henry DiTonti, who explored the Mississippi River Valley. Known as "Tonti the Iron Hand" because he lost a hand in battle, Henry DiTonti accompanied the Frenchman Robert La Salle in the first exploration of the Great Lakes aboard *The Griffin,* a ship he built in 1679. Tonti also founded the first European settlement in Illinois in 1680, and the first French settlement in Arkansas in 1683. He sailed under the French flag because he was from Gaeta, a town between Rome and Naples, which was originally controlled by France. Today the city of Tontitown in Arkansas is named in his honor. Alphonse Tonty, the younger brother of Henry, co-founded the city of Detroit, Michigan, in 1704 and served as its colonial governor for twelve years.

The route to the source of the Mississippi River was discovered in 1823 by Giacomo Costantino Beltrami while he was exploring the territory that later became Minnesota. In 1886 Minnesota created Beltrami County in honor of the explorer's discovery.

Right, above: Sebastian Cabot sailed to South America under the Spanish flag and claimed that continent for Spain.

Right, below: Filippo Mazzei, Thomas Jefferson's neighbor at Monticello, is credited with inspiring the Virginia statesman's phrase about equality in the Declaration of Independence. Although of Italian heritage, he was a true American patriot and drew up a plan to capture British troops in New York by cutting off their escape route to the sea.

THE AMERICAN REVOLUTION

Two key names come to mind when speaking of the Italian contribution to the war for independence: Filippo Mazzei and Francesco Vigo. Mazzei was a Florentine physician and merchant who had moved to England to import wine and olive oil from Italy. His friends Benjamin Franklin and Thomas Adams convinced him to come to Virginia to conduct agricultural experiments, and it is there that the Florentine intellectual met Thomas Jefferson, George Washington, and James Madison. A long-standing and close friendship with Jefferson, documented by letters the two men exchanged over the course of many years, was the deciding factor in his move to Virginia. From the time of his arrival in Monticello, where Jefferson had his home, Mazzei proved to be not only a friend but also a counselor and great source of ideas. For example, Jefferson's famous phrase "All men are created equal" was inspired by a passage from Mazzei's own writings : "All men are by nature equally free and independent."

The very name America is taken from Amerigo Vespucci, a skilled Italian navigator and mapmaker who sailed to the New World in 1499. He was the first to believe that Columbus had not reached the Indies but had actually discovered a new continent.

Another Italian in early U.S. history was Francesco Vigo, who dedicated himself to the cause of his adopted country without reserve. A rich and well-known merchant, he spent large sums of money to finance the American Revolutionary War effort, especially for the purchase of firearms. He is also believed to be the first Italian to be granted U.S. citizenship. However, this depth of patriotism for his new homeland cost him so dear that he died in poverty, having spent all his wealth for the cause of American independence. Some consolation was offered in 1786, when the new government awarded his heirs $50,000 as compensation.

William Paca of Maryland was one of two men of Italian descent who signed the Declaration of Independence. Caesar Rodney of Delaware was the other. Caesar Rodney, ailing and infirm, made a treacherous ride from Delaware to Philadelphia to vote for independence in 1776.

The Declaration of Independence promised freedoms that attracted Italians to the new republic.

THE REBELS OF '76. OR, THE FIRST ANNOUNCEMENT OF THE GREAT DECLARATION.

EXPLANATION.—It is sunset on the 4th of July, 1776. The members of the old Continental Congress, having signed the Declaration, are seen in the act of leaving the Hall of Independence. HANCOCK, distinguished by his dark dress, stands on the steps in front of the hall-door, announcing to a friend that the Declaration has just been signed. FRANKLIN is seen at his right, JEFFERSON leans against the right pillar of the door. ADAMS is conversing with Jefferson—between their heads is seen the face of LIVINGSTON, and against the left pillar stands ROGER SHERMAN. These form the group on the steps. We then commence on the left of the picture, and counting every figure, discover the following persons: 1, a citizen; 2, WILSON, a signer; 3, a citizen; 4, a tory; 5, a signer; 6, a lady; 7, her father; 8, the Indian who bore the Declaration to the camp of Washington; 9, Thomas Paine, talking with No. 10, Benjamin Rush, and 11, Robert Morris, both signers. Behind them the heads of citizens are seen, and to the right, a crowd of patriots, Quakers, tories, &c. eagerly disputing the nature and merits of the Declaration.

Entered according to act of Congress, in the year 1860, by S. Ashton in the Clerk's Office of the District Court of the U. S. for the Eastern District of Pennsylvania.

During the Revolutionary War, three regiments totaling fifteen hundred Italian soldiers fought alongside the Americans. Among the American officers were men of Italian descent, including Captain Cosimo de Medici and Colonel Richard Talliaferro. Two of the original signers of the Declaration of Independence were men of Italian origin: William Paca, one of the first senators and later governor of Maryland, and Caesar Rodney the future governor of Delaware, who rode seventy miles through a torrential rainstorm, despite being stricken with cancer, to vote for independence in 1776. Caesar Rodney's nephew and namesake, Caesar Augustus Rodney, also had a distinguished career in public service. He represented Delaware in both the House of Representatives and the Senate, served as attorney general under presidents Jefferson and Madison, and helped develop the Monroe Doctrine.

The year 1783 marked the end of the Revolutionary War and the beginning of a significant influx of Italian immigrants to the New World. For the most part, those newly arrived were tradesmen, artisans, musicians, and artists, but the mid-nineteenth century saw the arrival of many political refugees who had joined the Italian unification movement known as the Risorgimento. About ten thousand Italians who arrived in the United States during this period (1840–1860) fought in the bloodiest and most brutal conflict the nation had ever seen, the Civil War.

THE RISORGIMENTO

By the 1860s, both Italy and America were caught up in passionate struggles regarding nationhood. In Italy the revolutionary phase of the unification movement had begun with the insurrections of 1848 and 1849 led by Giuseppe Garibaldi, the great military commander of the Risorgimento. Garibaldi's charisma and determination made him an international hero whose name was known throughout Europe and in the Americas. Numerous foreign soldiers, including many Americans, enlisted as volunteers in Garibaldi's army to drive the Bourbons and Austrians out of Italy.

In the same way, thanks to a curious historic and cultural parallelism, many Italians, exiled from their homeland for their political activities and newly settled in the United States, enlisted in the Union Army because it represented the same cause—unification—that they had fought for in Italy. Some of the Italians who most distinguished themselves during the American Civil War were officers who

HISTORY

Giuseppe Garibaldi became the hero of the Italian reunification movement. He was offered a command in the Union Army by President Lincoln but declined. However, many of his followers took sides in the American Civil War. The Thirty-ninth New York Infantry was named the Garibaldi Guard in his honor. One hundred fifty of its 850 men were of Italian heritage.

had served with Garibaldi: Alberto Maggi served as commander of the Thirty-third Massachusetts Artillery, Achille Di Vecchi as a captain of the Tenth Massachusetts Light Artillery, and James R. Del Vecchio as quartermaster and later captain of the New York Enfants Perdues.

Two heroes of Garibaldi's revolution in Italy, Ercole Salvetti and Ambrogio Scopini, also joined the Union Army, as did Oliviero Bixio, brother of Garibaldi's famous general Nino Bixio, and Carlo Garibaldi, the Italian commander's own nephew, who was a soldier in the Sixteenth Massachusetts Infantry. Giuseppe Garibaldi was offered a command as major general in the Union Army by President Lincoln but declined. Still, to honor him, the Thirty-ninth New York Infantry was known as the Garibaldi Guard. It fought in the Union Army from Bull Run to Appomattox, and 150 of its men were Italian. More than one hundred Italian Americans served as officers in the Union forces, including four generals, two naval commanders, eleven naval officers, nine colonels and lieutenant colonels, and twenty-eight majors and captains. (The exact number is unknown because of the Americanization of Italian surnames and mixed marriages.) Four of the Italian-American generals who served during or after the Civil War were Luigi Palma di Cesnola, Enrico Fardella, Eduardo Ferrero, and Francis B. Spinola. General Ferrero of the Fifty-first New York Regiment was among the first Union officers to command black troops.

Union generals Luigi Palma di Cesnola and Francis Spinola received due honors for their contributions during the war. The former, a Piedmontese officer, was awarded the Congressional Medal of Honor and later became the first director of New York's Metropolitan Museum of Art. Spinola later was the first Italian American in Congress. He served from 1887 to 1891, representing New York City.

Italians fought in the Confederate Army as well. Over the course of the first four days of enlistment, 170 Italians joined the Southern ranks. In the end, the Italian troops serving under General Robert E. Lee numbered several thousand. Most of these hailed from Louisiana, while the others came from Alabama, Mississippi, Tennessee, and Florida. Some of these soldiers didn't even speak English, and the only command they understood was the order to attack.

Among the Italian-American officers in the Confederate Army were Captain Ernest Cucullu, commander of the Tenth Louisiana Infantry Zouaves, which

Above: Don Gentile, "the Ace of Aces," was a distinguished World War II pilot. As a captain in the U.S Army Air Force, he shot down more than thirty Nazi aircraft. He died tragically in a training accident in 1950 when he was only thirty years old.

Below: John Basilone, a U.S. Marine and hero at Guadalcanal in World War II, received the U.S. Congressional Medal of Honor and the Navy Cross. He died in the Battle of Iwo Jima in 1945.

counted twenty-seven Italians in its ranks, and the five Phinizi brothers (their name was an anglicization of Finizi), two of whom, Charles and Jacob, were regiment captains, and Captain Frank Arrighi, commander of the C and D companies of the Sixteenth Mississippi Infantry.

In the meantime, on the other side of the ocean, King Vittorio Emanuele II, accompanied by Garibaldi, made his triumphant entrance into Naples. The year was 1861, and Italy had finally become a united nation, at least geographically if not on the civil and economic levels. The differences in terms of economic resources and job opportunities between Northern and Southern Italy were still immense, and this triggered the greatest mass exodus of Italians the country had ever seen. Millions fled the peninsula for the United States between 1880 and 1920, raising the population of Italians in the United States to more than five million. Another ten million journeyed to Argentina, Brazil, and Canada, or to Russia, Germany, and other European countries.

BECOMING AMERICANS

The naturalization process for these immigrants was far from simple. To become Americans, Italians had to prove their loyalty and good faith toward their new homeland, and were often forced to pay a high price, facing deep-rooted prejudices, restrictions, suffering, humiliation, and discrimination. For many years during this wave of immigration, the Italian newcomers had fewer job opportunities and, more important, earned much less than American citizens.

Despite the brutality, death, and destruction it brings, war has the potential to unite a nation's people with a bond that is difficult to create in times of prosperity. History has shown us that, for a country to gain its identity, it has often been necessary for its people to share the same loss.

This was particularly true for the Italians and Italian Americans who fought in the U.S. armed forces during the two world wars.

In World War I, when Italy was an ally of the United States, more than 300,000 men, 12 percent of the entire U.S. Army, were Italian Americans, including 87,000 who were not yet citizens. Among them was Fiorello La Guardia, who was to become the first Italian-American mayor of New York City. At the end of the war, the losses proved to be grievous. Although at the time Italians comprised just 4 percent of the American population, they accounted for 10 percent of those who fell in combat. Despite this fact, a scornful and discriminatory attitude toward many ethnic groups, Italians included, continued to grow throughout the United States. Many immigrants were seen as inferior, or worse yet, as a disturbing force—as conspiratorial, subversive, or dangerous—often on the basis of vague and ill-founded considerations, as the trial and execution of Nicola Sacco and Bartolomeo Vanzetti showed. The two were tried and convicted of a robbery-murder for which no concrete evidence was presented. The trial went on for seven years and earned international interest, but to this day no one knows if they were guilty or not. On August 23, 1927, Sacco and Vanzetti were executed in the electric chair by the state of Massachusetts.

World War II finally allowed Italians to be assimilated into the American culture, but as always, there was a high price to pay. Almost 1.5 million Italians fought in the U.S. forces during World War II, in an army in which the total number of troops numbered twelve million.

During World War II an estimated 1.5 million Italian Americans fought for America and proved their heroism. One of the bravest was John Basilone, a Marine sergeant from New Jersey who fought alone for three days against an entire Japanese regiment at the Battle of Guadalcanal (1942), raised millions of dollars in war bonds, and was killed in action during the Battle of Iwo Jima in 1945. Basilone is the only enlisted Marine in U.S. history to receive the nation's two highest military honors for valor, the Navy Cross and the Congressional Medal of Honor, for his service in World War II.

Captain Don Gentile of the U.S. Army Air Force shot down more than thirty Nazi planes during World War II. Eisenhower called the twenty-four-year-old pilot a "one-man Air Force" and personally pinned the Distinguished Service Cross on him. Born in Ohio, the "Ace of Aces" died in a training accident after the war in 1950 when he was only thirty.

Despite hard-won praise and medals of honor, Italian Americans suffered civil-rights violations at the hands of the U. S. Department of Justice during the first year of the war. The Italians were considered enemies due to their native land's alliance with Germany and Japan, and were subjected to persecution at the hands of the U.S. government. A legislative measure that came into effect the night of December 11, 1941, and lasted for nearly a year labeled more than 600,000 foreign-born Italians as "enemy aliens." At least sixteen hundred were arrested, and about 250 were put in detention camps, and an estimated ten thousand were forced to move from cities situated mainly on the coasts to "safer" locations further inland. Others lost many of their rights and freedoms. They were subjected to curfews, had their homes searched and their cameras, radios, and other possessions confiscated. A number of Italians on both coasts were not allowed to travel more than five miles from their homes. One of these, a Sicilian fisherman, was unable to visit the San Francisco restaurant of his son, Joe DiMaggio.

Despite their early difficulties in gaining acceptance into American society, Italian Americans remained fiercely loyal to the country that had given them and their families so many opportunities. Evidence of their patriotism is found in this country's military history. At least thirty-nine Italian Americans have received the Congressional Medal of Honor. These include six in the Civil War, fourteen in World War II, and ten in the Vietnam War.

Today, at the beginning of a new millennium, Italian Americans have made remarkable contributions to this nation's life, in business, government, science, medicine, education, and law enforcement as well as in sports and entertainment. They came here seeking a better life and, having found it, made America a stronger nation as well.

A statue of John Basilone, erected in his home town, Raritan, New Jersey.

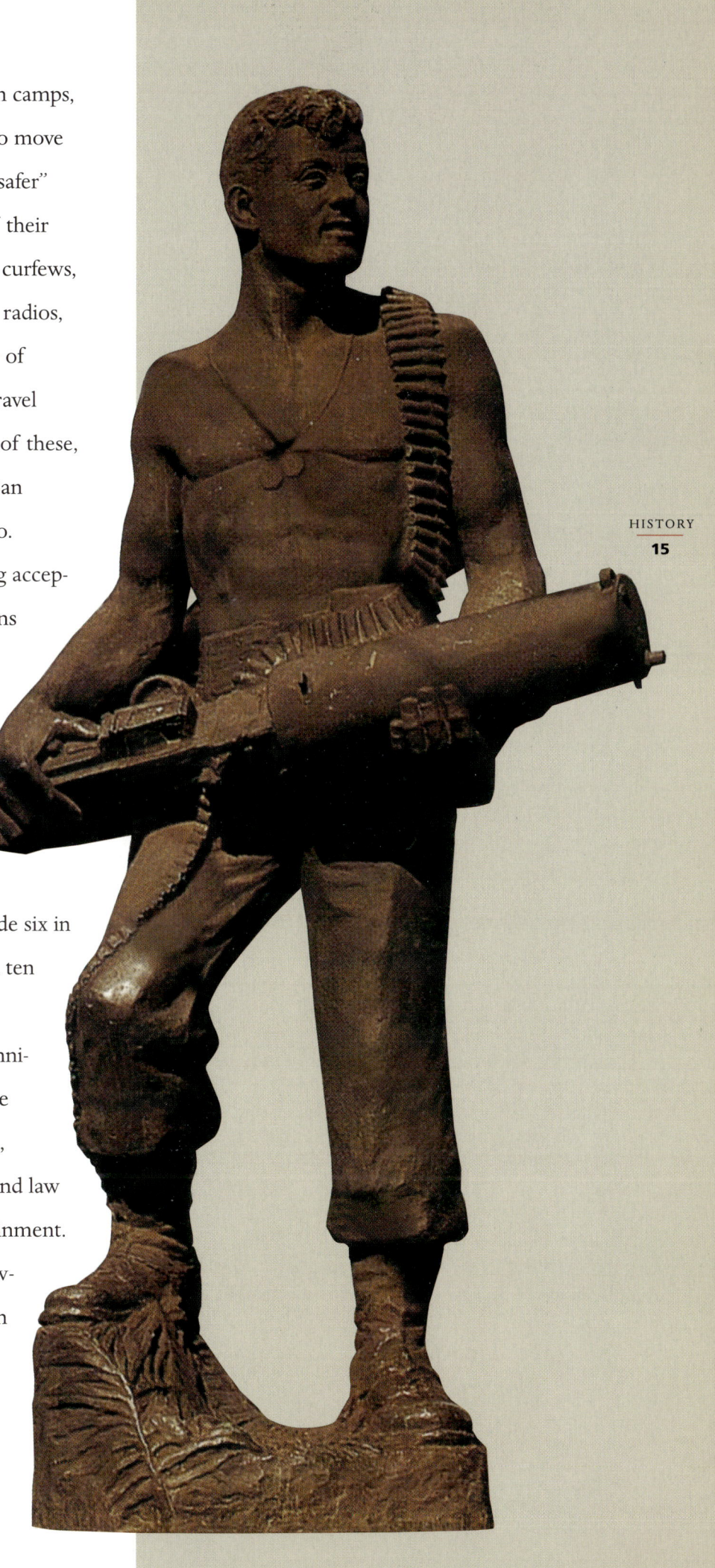

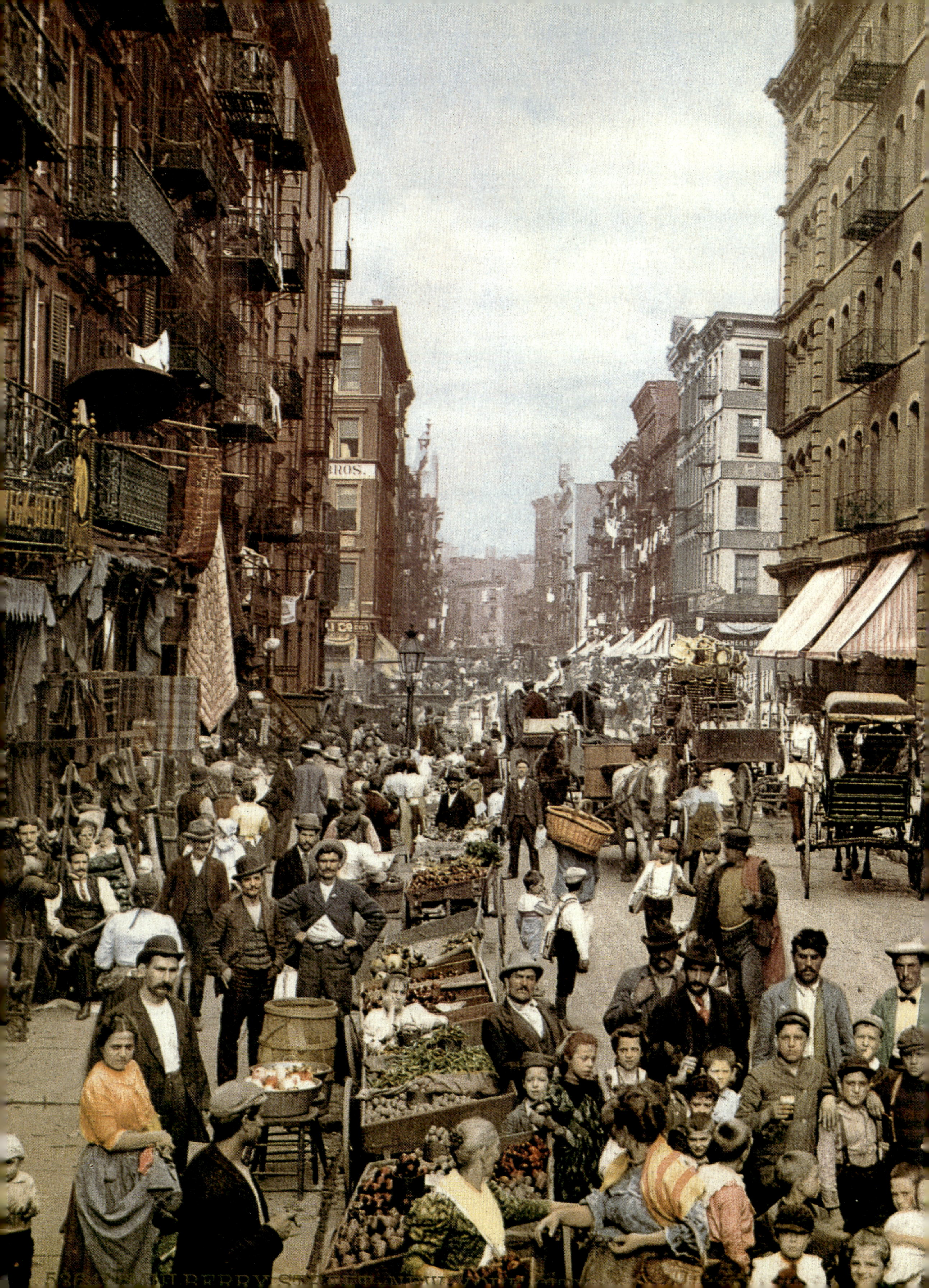
BROS.

PURSUING THE DREAM

THE GREAT MIGRATION

Between 1870 and 1920 fifteen million Italians left their native land for foreign countries. Five million of these headed toward the Americas, particularly the United States and Argentina, but many others chose to go to Australia or Canada, or to Russia, Germany, and other European countries. This exodus began just a few years after the unification of Italy, despite all the growth and prosperity a unified Italy seemed to promise. Ironically, the birth of the Italian nation acted as a catalyst for mass flight. What happened to cause this unprecedented event?

To answer this question, one could begin by studying the statistics regarding the Italians who were leaving the peninsula. About 80 percent of the immigrants came from the south, and most of these were males between eighteen and forty-five years of age, and in the prime of their strength. Many were peasants and farmers; others were artisans and unskilled workers. Until the reunification, Southern Italians had been governed by the Bourbons, an Italian branch of Spanish nobility who were considered unbearable and arrogant tyrants because they cared nothing for the interests of the people. The Southern Italians saw unification, which freed them of Bourbon rule, as an opportunity to improve their situation drastically and break free from the yoke of poverty that had held them for centuries.

This early photograph of Mulberry Street shows the heart of New York's Little Italy. Mulberry Street is located on Manhattan's Lower East Side and at the turn of the century was a bustling market as well as the destination for many immigrants, who fled the poverty of southern Europe.

Above: The Statue of Liberty, seen with the ships of New York Bay in the background.

Right: The Statue of Liberty has long been a symbol of freedom for the Italian immigrants to the United States.

Southern Italy had always been a land subject to foreign invasions. Some conquerors, such as the Normans who established themselves in Sicily during the Middle Ages, brought prosperity to the regions they colonized. Under the rule of Frederick II, for example, the city of Palermo was a capital of economy and trade, a true European court attracting artists, philosophers, and writers. Long before this, the Greeks had transformed Syracuse (also in Sicily) into a powerful city and a crossroads for the world's trade routes and cultures. Not all of the invaders, however, were so benevolent. Some, such as the Saracens or the Bourbons, brought chaos and suffering to Southern Italy, sacking, destroying, and pillaging every resource the land had to offer.

As a consequence of foreign rule, Southern Italians never had the chance to establish their own identity, having been forced time after time to adapt themselves to the various foreign cultures that invaded their land. They began to believe that subordination was the only way to survive. With thousands of years of subjugation at their backs, it is no wonder that the Southern Italians were so full of hope and expectation at the prospect of the Risorgimento. For the first

PURSUING
THE DREAM

19

PURSUING
THE DREAM

20

time in centuries, they were offered freedom and the power to control their own destinies.

They saw Giuseppe Mazzini and Giuseppe Garibaldi, the two fathers of the Risorgimento, as their heroic saviors. Garibaldi in particular, with his simplicity and charisma, had won the sympathy and loyalty of many Sicilians and Calabrians, who saw him as the man capable of dismantling the feudal system into which they had been forced for centuries. The Mille, the thousand volunteer soldiers in red shirts whom Garibaldi assembled in the name of patriotism and unification, were victorious against all odds, pushing the Bourbon army gradually northward until it was defeated by the Piedmontese troops of King Vittorio Emanuele. Garibaldi met the king in Teano, near Caserta, and when they shook hands the unification of Italy was sealed.

Unfortunately, the changes that people had hoped unification would bring were not quick in coming, at least not in Southern Italy. For the peasants there, who were anxious for economic change and relief from centuries of subjugation, the government in Turin revealed itself to be no more than the latest in a long succession of conquerors bent on exploiting an already impoverished land.

The economic policies the Turin government put in place after the unification called for new taxes to finance the nation's development. It was unavoidable that the peasants in Southern Italy, who were so poor that many did not have one full meal a day, began to see these policies as a penalty and to harbor hatred for the government that enforced them. In the end the Italian government came to be considered a worse tyrant than the Bourbons, especially as far as taxation was concerned. Under Bourbon rule, there had been regulations exempting those close to total poverty from paying taxes. The Italian government's new economic order, however, required the peasants to pay taxes on all their possessions, even the tools they needed for work. There was even a tax on mules. But there was no tax on the cattle belonging to wealthy landowners. These and other government policies widened the already enormous gap between Northern and Southern Italy, between the government and the people. Eventually the situation became volatile. The Turin government in Piedmont heard and believed reports of the peasants', and especially the Sicilians', "rebellious" attitude as well as rumors of insurrection. Eventually it sent an army to Sicily to control the situation and put an end to any protest. By now the population of Southern Italy despaired of

The Immigrant Station at Ellis Island received millions of Italians early in the twentieth century. Those immigrants blocked from entry—mostly for health reasons—were sent back on the next ship.

X-28

Left, above: Life was difficult for many people who remained in Italy during World War I, such as these children who waited for bread in Pordenone.

Left, below: Washing fruits and vegetables at a public spigot in Rome, 1919.

Above: Italian earthquake refugees aboard the ship that would take them to the United States. Homeless and with little hope of recovering what they had lost, these immigrants looked to America as the "Land of Opportunity."

Photographer Lewis Hine documented the arrival of this Italian family at Ellis Island in 1905.

finding any hope in the promises of the new nation, and some citizens chose the path of brigandage. The brigands were violent and mysterious figures, for the most part men reduced to ruin, who had nothing left to lose. They lived in the forests and fed their families by robbing and stealing. Their protest was an open challenge to the government and a last, desperate effort before the inevitable self-imposed exile from their homeland.

In 1870, with the annexing of Rome, Italy's unification finally became official, and thousands of Italians began to abandon their homes, families, and land. In addition to a profoundly bitter sense of resignation, they felt a strong anger for King Vittorio Emanuele, the new "foreigner" who was forcing them deeper into poverty. As they left their cities, they continued to sing the praises of their hero Garibaldi, who, like them, had witnessed the betrayal of his dreams and hopes for the Italy he had helped to unite. Hundreds of thousands fled, leaving behind almost all their possessions. With little baggage and only their dreams of a better life to give them strength, entire families faced the trying journey to the

PURSUING
THE DREAM
25

Above: A pasta restaurant on a Neapolitan street, circa 1903.

Overleaf: This crowded block in Lower Manhattan was home to thousands of Italians in the early twentieth century. Within a generation, however, many worked their way out of these tenements and into the "suburbs" of Brooklyn, Queens, and the Bronx.

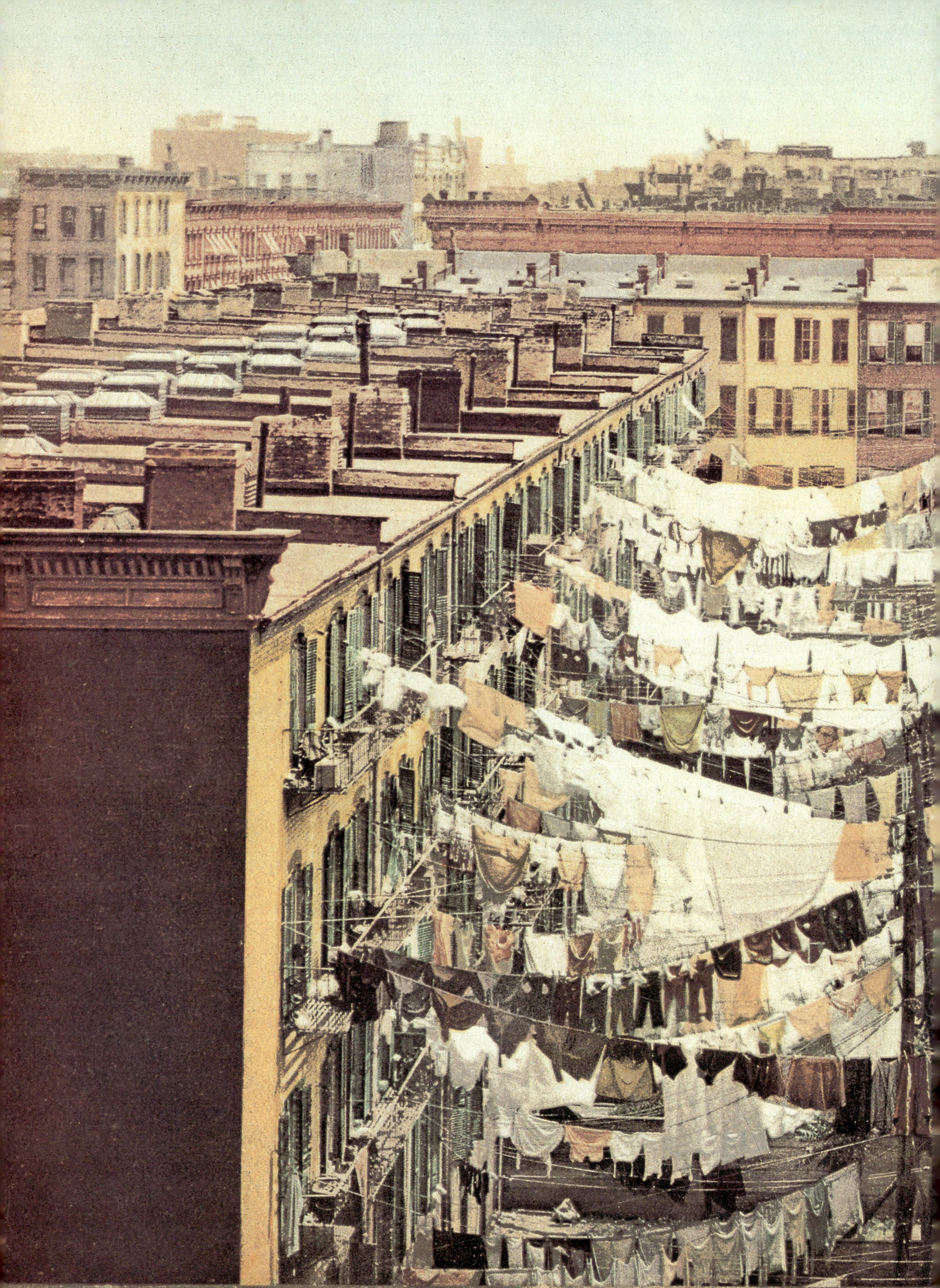

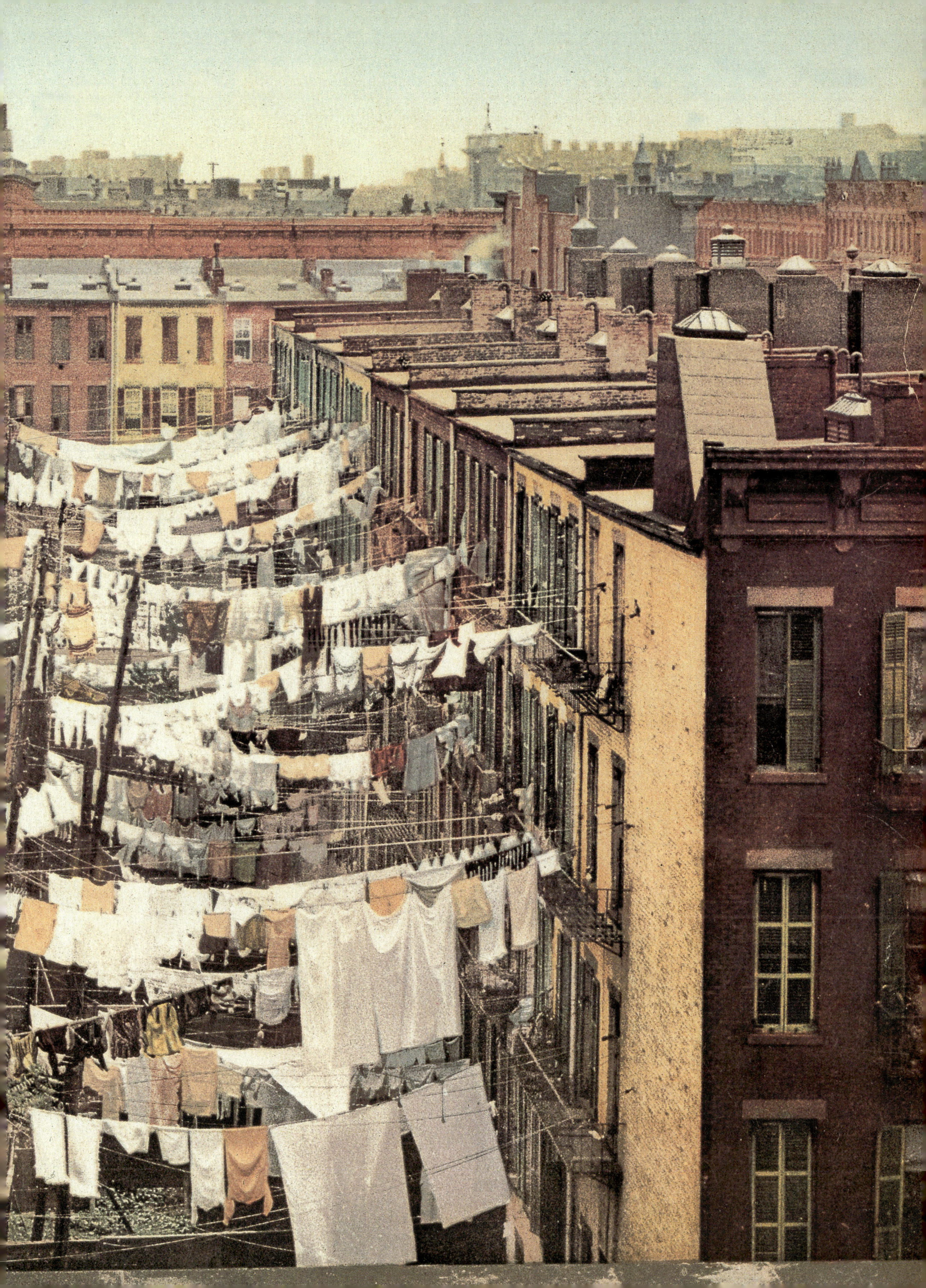

PURSUING
THE DREAM

28

James Cesare, Jack Porcello, and Jack Cesare were among the many people who brought a strong musical heritage with them from Italy.

Italian port cities where they would embark for America. The name America stood for all that many of these Italians had long yearned for. Myth and reality blended in the tales of those who had already arrived on the other side of the ocean, describing that continent as a land of opportunity where the people were kind and there was plenty of work for everyone and a chance of prosperity.

What was it that fueled this dream that many Italians chose to follow? First of all, the tales of those who had gone to the United States, which persuaded even the most doubtful. Those travelers returned home changed, well-dressed, groomed, and with money in their pockets. They told relatives and friends of a rich and promising land where they had found work easily. Seeing this transformation was enough to convince most to try to set out for America and, leaving their families with a promise to send for them from the new land, they set sail.

Everyone has seen the famous photographs of hundreds of immigrants packed into the steerage sections of ships with deplorable sanitary conditions. The faces in these photos bear the expression of a bewildered people's degradation, a people tempered by desperation and exhaustion who had somehow found the will and strength to start over, often creating tales of incredible success from nothing. Whole families later joined husbands, fathers, friends, or countrymen, and often upon their reunion in the United States they re-created the neighborhoods they had left behind in Italy. One of the most striking examples of this phenomenon took place in New York City. As the port of arrival, New York was the first place the immigrants considered as a possible new home. So many Italians settled in Lower Manhattan that they created a Little Italy. Many such communities later sprang up in other cities with dense Italian populations. These neighborhoods were a reconstruction on a smaller scale of the towns in Southern Italy the immigrants had come from. Finding themselves alone in a land where the language, customs, food, and traditions were completely foreign, the newcomers tended to stick together, thus creating a less hostile and more familiar environment for themselves.

Hundreds of thousands of immigrants, attracted by the rumors of job opportunities, journeyed north or west, settling in Rochester, Buffalo, Philadelphia, Boston, and various cities along the East Coast, as well as in cities and towns in the South, West and Midwest. The flow of Italians seemed endless: In only ten years (from 1900 to 1910), two million Italians arrived in the United

Sebastiano and Innocenza Fede were called Sam and Annie by their American friends in Birmingham, Alabama. They are seen here in an early twentieth-century photograph with their two daughters, Jennie (left) and Jeanette (right). After coming to Birmingham from Sicily, Mr. Fede worked in the coal mines. He eventually owned his own grocery business.

States, and another 2.5 million would establish themselves before 1930. There was a brief hiatus around 1923, when federal authorities, alarmed by the ever-swelling flood of immigrants from southern and eastern Europe, introduced regulations aimed to reduce the number of new arrivals from these areas.

Three quarters of the five million Italians who poured into the United States settled in the Northeast, forming Italian communities in many major cities. But Italian communities formed in the Deep South as well. Two of the biggest were in New Orleans, Louisiana, and Birmingham, Alabama. The tens of thousands who decided to settle in Southern cities worked mostly as coal miners. Many rich deposits of coal or other materials had been discovered in the second half of the nineteenth century, and there was a large demand for unskilled workers. Although the concentration of Italians was highest in industrial areas, all the states became home to Italian communities of varying sizes.

Today, according to the latest census, the number of people of Italian origin residing in the United States has reached about twenty million, establishing Italian Americans as the fifth largest ethnic group in this country. The figure is truly surprising considering that the entire population of Italy is no larger than sixty million. It clearly illustrates the dramatic proportions of an exodus that changed the history and destiny of both Italy and United States forever.

PURSUING
THE DREAM

31

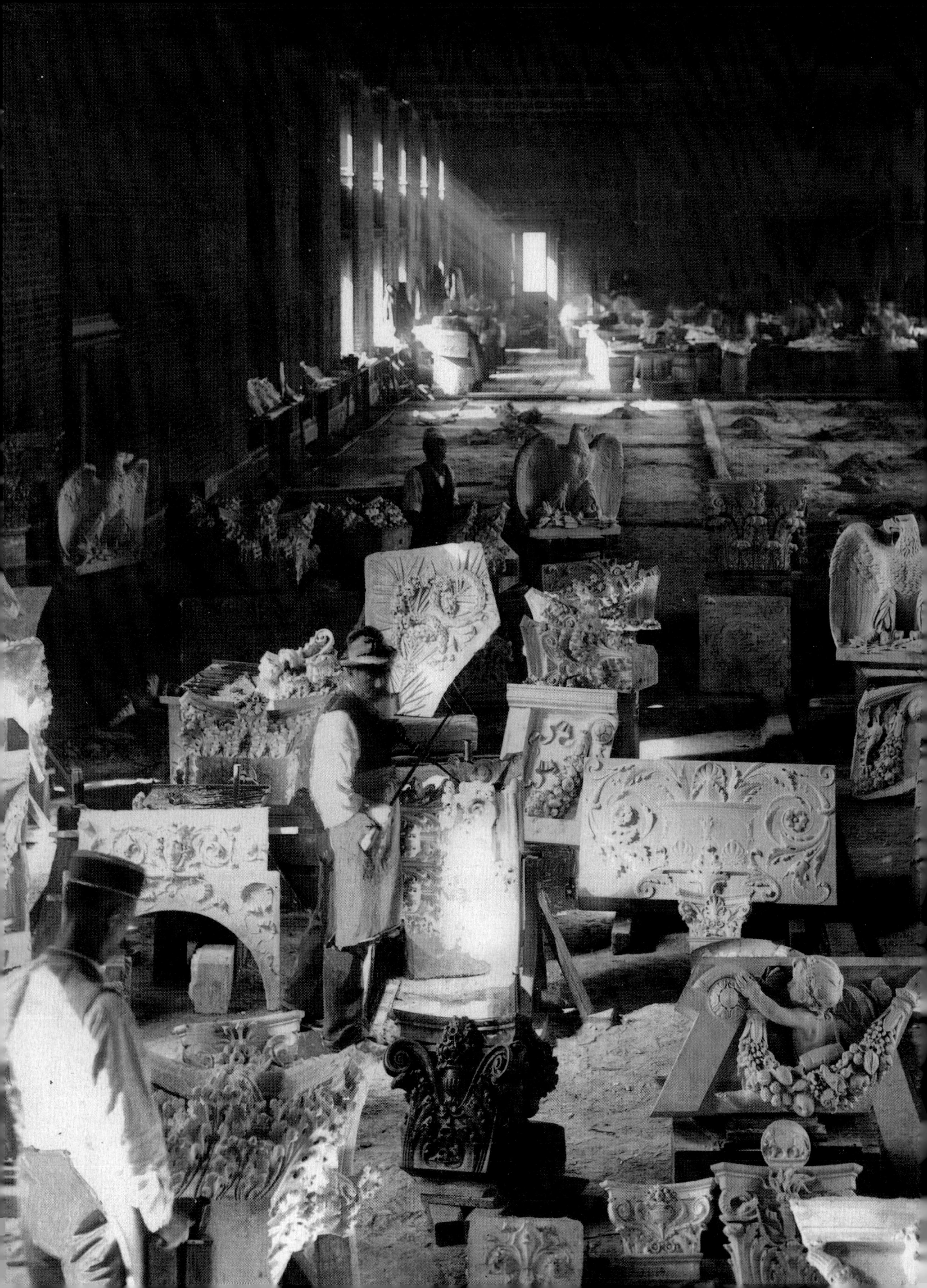

SUFFERING AND SACRIFICE

♦

ASCENDING THE SOCIAL LADDER

The millions of Italians who arrived in America at the beginning of the twentieth century faced the difficult task of creating something from nothing. Suffering and sacrifice were their constant companions during their first years in America. Their savings barely served to pay for passage to the United States, leaving them with enough to survive only a few months in the New World. This state of affairs made them easy prey for *padroni*, men who recruited workers sometimes directly from Italy, luring them to the United States with false promises of wealth and privilege, only to exploit them. Upon their arrival, the immigrants were completely at the mercy of the *padroni*, who provided them with contacts and operated as intermediaries during negotiations with possible employers. The Italians, who knew neither the language nor the customs of this new land, were completely helpless. The *padroni* often forced their "wards" to give them a significant part of their weekly pay, and sometimes demanded as much as 60 percent for their dubious services.

Many Italians' first impressions and experiences of America were far from positive. Among the services they promised and provided, the *padroni* took care of finding "decent" lodgings for new arrivals. For the most part, these lodgings were run-down, overcrowded apartments with poor sanitary conditions and no hot water, often without heating in the winter and ventilation in the summer. The extreme example of this situation was the neighborhood in New York that at the turn of the century was called Mulberry Bend. Centered in the lower part of Manhattan

Many craftsmen, such as these marble carvers from Pietrasanta, Italy, brought their skills with them to America.

SUFFERING
AND SACRIFICE

34

around Mulberry Street, this area became the heart of New York's Little Italy. By 1910 the estimated population density on Manhattan's Lower East Side was 290,000 people per square mile, reaching its highest concentration in Mulberry Bend. Entire blocks were home to mostly male workers, many of whom were Sicilians, who slept twelve to a small room. There were apartments that housed as many as five families, each one numbering an average of four or five members. Hundreds of thousands of other immigrants in the Little Italy communities of Boston, Chicago, Baltimore, and Philadelphia lived in similar conditions during the same period.

Despite the almost unbearable circumstances in which they were forced to live, the Italian immigrants refused to give up. The fact that they had survived exploitation and poverty in their homeland had surely hardened their resolve, enabling them to patiently build a future of dignity and to improve their social and economic prospects. Their strongest asset, apart from their tenacity, was their ability to save what little they had. Putting away at least 25 percent of their daily earnings, many Italians were able to make it through the most trying and

Left: Many poor immigrant women and their children performed menial jobs, such as making flower wreaths, just to survive. In this photo from 1912, Mrs. Mortaria and her four children, ages four to thirteen, work out of their tenement home.

Above: Men and boys sit outside a store during a festival in New York's Little Italy, circa 1908.

Around the turn of the century, children were employed as breaker boys in the mines, working in unhealthy and oppressive conditions. The children pictured here worked in the Kohinor mine, Shenandoah City, Pennsylvania, circa 1890.

humiliating times. Some of them, such as those who settled in the South and especially in New Orleans, were able to profit from the fruit trade or other areas of local commerce, finally reaching a higher social and economic status.

Nevertheless, earning a living in America was a hard and even tragic task for many. The men employed to build the railroads worked long hours, performing backbreaking labor for very poor wages. Moreover, in many cases these workers had to pay a percentage of their wages either to the agent who had recruited them or to the very company for which they worked. Many, for example, were forced to pay a rental fee for their work tools. In the worst scenarios, these men were even forced to buy daily meals from the company for at least five times their worth.

LIFE IN THE MINES

Hardship was common for Italian immigrants in all labor situations, and their difficulties were similar to those faced by other ethnic groups, but miners were certainly among those who suffered most. The mining industry was one of the nation's most powerful, and the mine owners exploited men who were willing to work in deplorable conditions for minimal wages. Demand for Italians was high because they had skills, such as stonecutting, which were lacking in America at the time—so thousands of them went to work in the mines of Colorado, Utah, Pennsylvania, Idaho, and Minnesota, situated in tiny, isolated towns owned by their employers.

Between 1870 and 1914 a great number of Italian, Greek, Polish, and Russian immigrants came to the mines of Colorado. The mines were so rich in coal deposits that they easily provided job opportunities. Hundreds of Italian immigrants found work with one of the largest coal mining companies in the state, Colorado Fuel & Iron (CF&I), owned by John D. Rockefeller. Working conditions were unbearable, and there was no regard for the miners' safety or the camps' sanitary conditions. Typhoid was a common disease due to the lack of clean water, and according to a study from that period the disease killed an average of 150 men every year. Furthermore, the work of a miner was constantly fraught with the risk of accidents and explosions in the mine. Between 1902 and 1917 there were twelve explosions in CF&I camps, and 474 miners lost their lives. These explosions resulted from the high concentration of coal dust in the air. In order to minimize expenses, CF&I never took the precaution of spraying the mines. Later, the company wrote off most of the explosions as the consequence of worker negligence.

THE LUDLOW MASSACRE

The exploitation and abuse in the mines only reached the attention of the general public after an incident in which twenty-three men, women, and children, of whom eleven were Italian, lost their lives. It would go down in history as the Ludlow Massacre. The events that led to this tragedy began in 1913 with a strike. The Colorado miners, tired of their terrible working conditions, had presented a series of requests, including a 10 percent increase in wages, a limit of eight hours of work per day, and the freedom to reject company housing. The United Mine Workers of America acted as the mediator for their requests. On September 13, 1913, more than twelve thousand men with their wives and children left their jobs and homes at CF&I and moved into tents provided by the union. The tension between the miners and the company increased. CF&I placed numerous armed guards around the camps and installed spotlights for nighttime surveillance.

This situation continued for months until it reached its tragic conclusion on April 20, 1914, when heavy gunfire broke out between miners and armed guards. Firearms and torches bombarding the Ludlow camp set fire to the tents housing the miners' families. In trenches beneath the tents, dug by the miners themselves to protect their families in case of attack, dozens of people were trapped in the deadly blaze. The next day, twenty-three corpses were found, and the news made headlines throughout the world. The United States Commission on Industrial Relations opened a fruitless inquiry that was unable to determine the actual number of people who lost their lives that day. In the end no one was arrested and not a single company representative was implicated in the massacre. In spite of this tragedy, the miners' requests were ignored, and working conditions did not improve until 1932, when the Norris–La Guardia Act was passed. This law banned the so-called Yellow Dog contracts, which obligated workers to accept the worst possible treatment without the possibility of asking for raises or better conditions. Most important, the law strengthened workers' rights to form unions.

After World War II, the situation of all Italian immigrants in Colorado

SUFFERING AND SACRIFICE

39

Above: The Massachusetts Militia was called in to guard the factory entrance during a strike at the textile mills in Lawrence, Massachusetts, 1912.

Below: In this scene of protestors at the Philadelphia Streetcar strike in 1910, rioters are charging a car on Kensington Avenue. Italian Americans were active in establishing many U.S. labor unions.

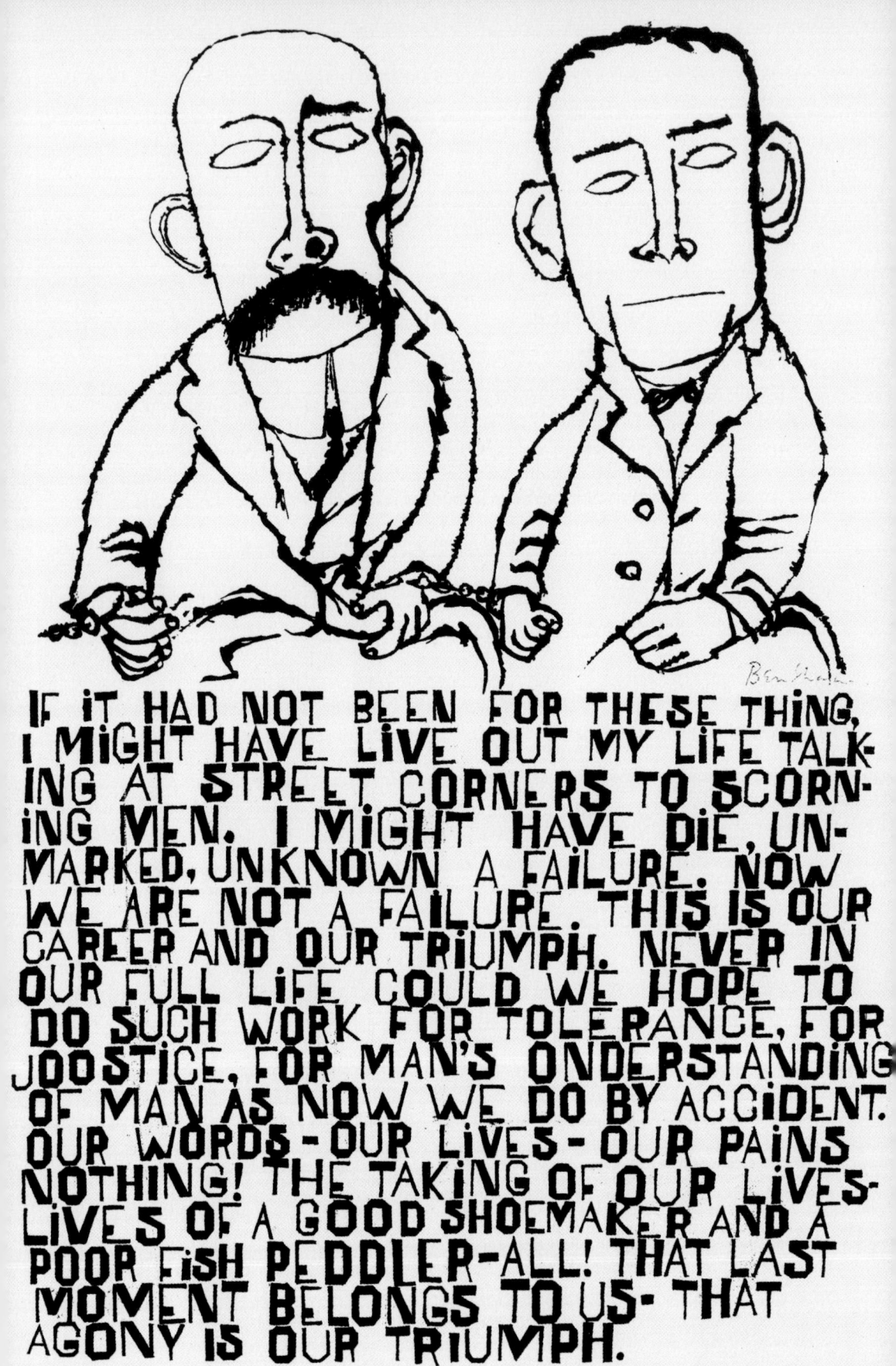

IF IT HAD NOT BEEN FOR THESE THING, I MIGHT HAVE LIVE OUT MY LIFE TALKING AT STREET CORNERS TO SCORNING MEN. I MIGHT HAVE DIE, UNMARKED, UNKNOWN A FAILURE. NOW WE ARE NOT A FAILURE. THIS IS OUR CAREER AND OUR TRIUMPH. NEVER IN OUR FULL LIFE COULD WE HOPE TO DO SUCH WORK FOR TOLERANCE, FOR JOOSTICE, FOR MAN'S ONDERSTANDING OF MAN AS NOW WE DO BY ACCIDENT. OUR WORDS - OUR LIVES - OUR PAINS NOTHING! THE TAKING OF OUR LIVES - LIVES OF A GOOD SHOEMAKER AND A POOR FISH PEDDLER - ALL! THAT LAST MOMENT BELONGS TO US - THAT AGONY IS OUR TRIUMPH.

began to improve significantly. In the areas of Trinidad, Starkville, and Pueblo, Italians formed communities and opened various types of businesses. Some families were eventually able to save enough money to purchase their own land outside the towns and dedicate themselves to farming.

ITALIANS IN THE UNIONS

The Italian contribution to creating better working conditions throughout the United States was fundamental. Among the Italian and Italian-American union leaders were Joseph Ettor, who was recruited to lead the Industrial Workers of the World (IWW) at twenty-seven years of age, and his friend, the poet and journalist Arturo Giovannitti, who had been convinced by Ettor to participate in the historic strike against the Lawrence textile company. Carlo Tresca, an Italian anarchist who had fled political persecution in his homeland, later joined the Lawrence cause.

Lawrence, Massachusetts, was the heart of the American textile industry and home to the American Woolen Company, a company with thirty thousand employees, among whom Italians, numbering seventeen thousand, were the largest ethnic group. The incident that sparked the strike was a wage cut following the passing of a Massachusetts law that reduced weekly working hours from fifty-six to fifty-four for women and for children under eighteen years of age. On January 12, 1912, when they learned of the decrease in wages, all the male and female workers walked away from their workplaces in a spontaneous strike, cutting machine belts and breaking windows as they left. A few days later, twenty thousand workers filled the streets in what was to be the beginning of the longest and most terrible labor deadlock in the history of the United States.

Ettor and Giovannitti organized many of the picket lines and strongly supported the strikers. Three weeks into the dispute, the two were arrested, charged as accomplices in the fatal shooting of a young woman during one of the pickets. This trumped-up charge was designed to break the will of the strikers and organizers, but upon hearing of the imprisonment of Ettor and Giovannitti, a contingent of strikers led by Italians became even more determined to fight. They sent their children to stay with friends or relatives in other cities to spare them the hardship and hunger caused by the strike. Newspapers across the country showed front-page photographs of the tired and hungry children arriving at their

Artist Ben Shahn produced this poster to commemorate the unjust trial and subsequent execution of Nicola Sacco and Bartolomeo Vanzetti in 1927.

destinations, and a shocked public quickly took the side of the strikers. Ettor and Giovannitti were tried and acquitted later in the year, after a labor settlement had been reached. In the end, the strike had yielded positive results, and the company was forced to meet the workers' requests—above all a 15 percent raise in wages.

The Italians who helped build the New York City subway system came together to form one of the largest unions of immigrants in America. They, too, had requested raises, shorter workdays, and better conditions, and organized what would be remembered as the Lexington Avenue subway strike. The negotiations with their employers were conducted by Salvatore Ninfo, a twenty-one-year-old Sicilian who spoke English well enough to explain the workers' needs and requests, which were met within a short time.

Another important strike that helped America lay the foundations for an eight-hour workday and better conditions was the 1913 Paterson Silk Strike in New Jersey, during which 25,000 workers walked out of the silk mills. Two Italians, Maria Botto and her husband, Pietro, opened the doors of their home in Haledon, New Jersey, to the workers as a gesture of solidarity. The twelve-room Victorian-style house owned by the Bottos became the strikers' headquarters and today it houses the American Labor Museum, a national landmark.

WORKING WOMEN

Italian women also paid a high price to achieve better working conditions. Thousands worked in the textile industry—exploited, underpaid, and at times subjected to sexual abuse by their managers or supervisors in order to keep their jobs. Some were victims of accidents caused by faulty machinery that their employers did not care to repair. The worst episode in American history involving Italian women in the workplace was certainly the fire at the Triangle Shirtwaist Company, which occurred on March 25, 1911 in New York City. In a company that employed five hundred people, almost all women and children, the fire claimed the lives of 146 laborers, seventy-five of whom were Italian. This shocking death toll was due to the fact that the employers had blocked all the exits of the building to make sure that the women and girls could not take breaks during working hours. Many women jumped to their death from open windows. In December 1911 the owners of the company, Max Blanck and Isaac Harris, went

A funeral procession for those killed in the Triangle Shirtwaist Company fire, 1911.

on trial for manslaughter—and were acquitted.

The establishment of a union to protect the rights of women employed in the textile industry was the result of the efforts of an Italian-American woman named Angela Bambace, a worker at a shirtwaist company in the early twentieth century. At only eighteen years of age, she managed to unite a substantial number of her coworkers and form chapters or "locals" of the International Ladies' Garment Workers' Union (ILGWU) in New York and Maryland. In 1956 Bambace was elected vice president of the union—an unusual position, considering that until then the ILGWU had always been led by men—and she continued in that role until 1972, when she retired at more than seventy years of age.

Exploitation in the workplace and its sad results are only one aspect of the hardship Italian immigrants faced. Lynchings and other brutal crimes of prejudice still live in the memory of the Italian-American community. One of the

Right, above: James Pompey came to America in the 1920s on the advice of his brother. In this photo from 1942, the Italian-American farmer plows his field in Southington, Connecticut.

Right, below: Fishermen of Italian descent prepare bait and mend nets and traps at Fisherman's Wharf on San Francisco Bay, circa 1940.

worst episodes took place in New Orleans, where eleven Sicilians were lynched in 1891 by an enraged crowd that suspected them of the murder of a police officer who was investigating Mafia activities. All eleven had been found innocent at trial, but were murdered as a result of widespread prejudice, especially against Southern Italians—and Sicilians in particular. Sicilians were believed to have brought the feuds, knifings, and other rituals related to the Mafia phenomenon to America and, in so doing, to have threatened and lowered the quality of life in the United States. Other lynchings took place in Louisiana, Mississippi, and Colorado, sometimes following fights between Sicilians stemming from personal arguments such as jealousy or economic rivalry.

This history of suffering endures in the memories and family lore of many Italian Americans: Today the children and grandchildren of the miners of Colorado, the Vermont stonecutters and marble workers, the textile workers of New England, the railroad laborers, and all those who participated in the workers' struggles, live in a more democratic and civil country thanks in part to the contribution of their parents and grandparents. Today they have access to every professional field the nation has to offer, and indeed they often occupy leading positions, as we will see in the chapters that follow.

SUFFERING
AND SACRIFICE

45

FERRARA
EST. 1892
Ferrara
HOLY CANNOLI
FERRARA
FERRARA
FERRARA
FERRARA
FERRARA

BUSINESS AND ENTREPRENEURS

It is difficult to imagine the growth of America's industries and economy without the contribution of Italian Americans. From the infrastructure of roads, bridges, railroads, and subways that millions of immigrants helped to build to the food and wine industries and the thousands of large and small businesses founded and run by Italian Americans, the United States has much to thank Italy for.

One of the world's largest banks would not exist, nor would millions of products that Italian Americans invented and introduced to the market. An American institution, the shopping mall, would not exist, and people would have to do without Jacuzzis, fireworks, coffee machines, the three-way light bulb, cough drops, and the pizza, pasta, and canned sauces that have become staples of the American diet. Ice cream would only be served in cups if it weren't for Italo Marcioni, who invented the cone, and no one would ever have tasted one of America's most popular hamburgers, the Big Mac, had it not been invented by Jim Delligatti.

By the year 2000, the heads of the three largest stock exchanges in the United States were Italian American, as were many stockbrokers, financial analysts, and money managers. Entrepreneurs of Italian descent have also founded very successful national magazines, such as *Mirabella* and *Talk,* and, thanks to Steve Geppi's Diamond Comics, are leaders in the distribution of comic books throughout the world. Three generations of children have played with the popular Radio Flyer wagon, one of America's favorite toys, invented by an Italian-American cabinetmak-

The Ferrara Bakery has been a landmark in New York's Little Italy for more than a hundred years.

John F. Mariani, Jr., seated, and his brother, Harry Mariani, standing, own the Castello Banfi vineyards.

er, Antonio Pasin. Two of America's largest chains of bookstores, Barnes & Noble and Borders, are run by Leonard Riggio and Robert Di Romualdo respectively.

Today the U.S. economy counts on almost twenty million people of Italian descent who, with their efforts and successes, help it to run smoothly. Their presence has had an inestimable importance in making this country the greatest industrialized nation in the world.

EARLY ENTREPRENEURS

From colonial times, Italians who came to the New World rolled up their sleeves and enacted concrete plans to improve their personal, professional, and financial situations, thus contributing to the well-being of American society. One of these was Filippo Mazzei, who, although he is remembered mostly for his political contributions to the American Revolution, also launched an import business that focused principally on Italian wines.

Mazzei was a Florentine physician and merchant who came to the United States to carry out a study of the terrain and climatic conditions. Here he met such influential personages as future president Thomas Jefferson, who invited Mazzei to become his neighbor, giving him a piece of land on his estate, Monticello, so that he could build his home. On the surrounding land Mazzei cultivated vegetables, grape vines, and other products of which Jefferson became very fond. Mazzei summoned wine experts from Italy to cultivate the grapes around Monticello and throughout Virginia.

Unfortunately, the imminent Revolutionary War, combined with the harsh climate of the East Coast, which damaged many of the new vineyards, prevented Mazzei from establishing a solid wine business in the New World. He had a vision that America would one day become home to the world's most productive wine market, and if he had lived to see what Italian Americans have accomplished in this sector, he would know that his predictions were correct.

As wine producers, Italian Americans have reached the most admirable levels of prestige and experience. One of the major advantages of the millions of Italians who immigrated to the United States was their skill for working the land and producing wine. This knowledge allowed them to become leaders in the thriving California wine industry, which today generates billions of dollars in sales.

California was the geographic ideal for this industry, since its climate and

BUSINESS AND
ENTREPRENEURS

49

The Mondavi vineyard in California was founded by Robert Mondavi, whose parents originally came from the Marche region of Italy.

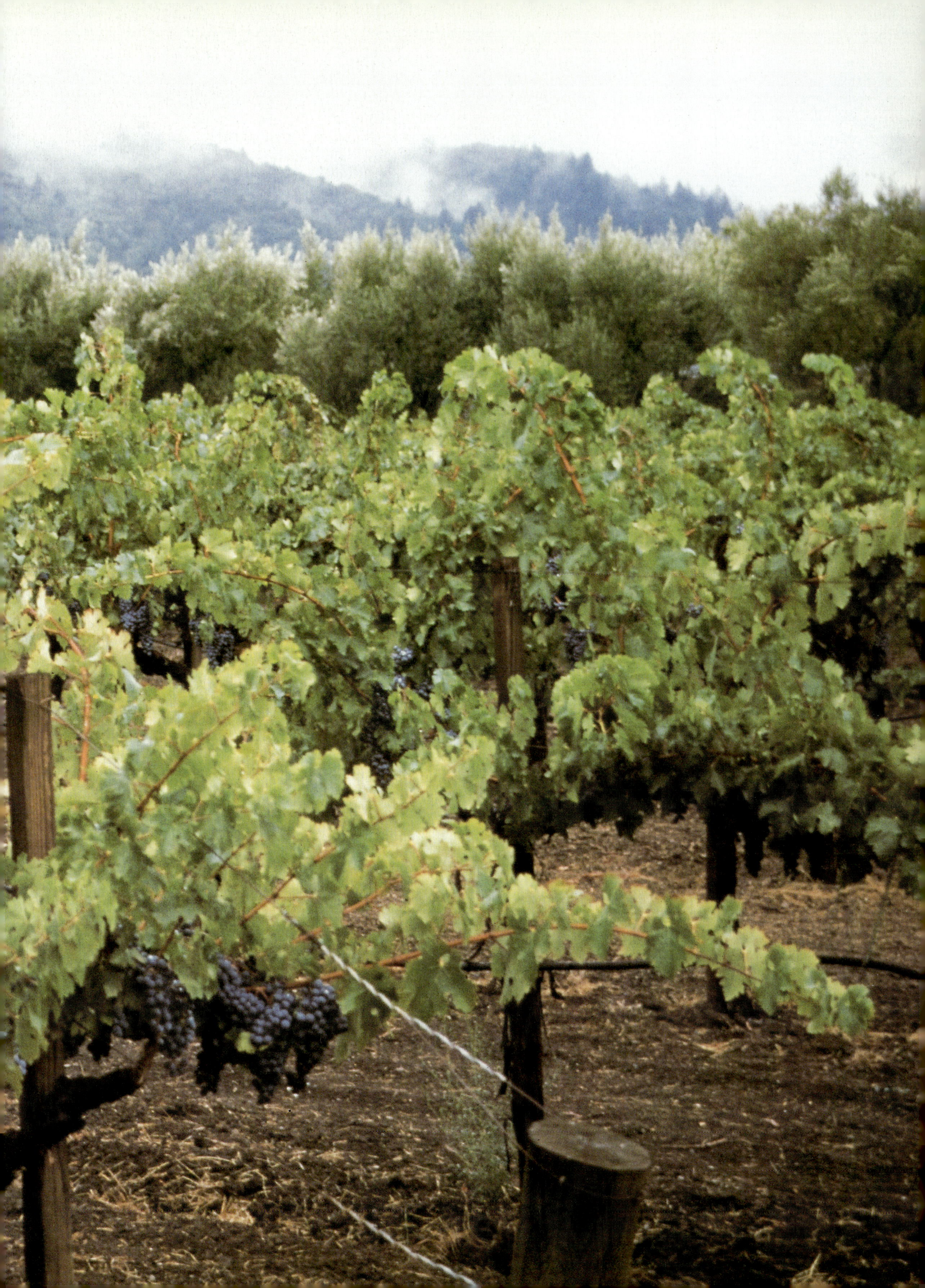

terrain were very similar to those of the Italian immigrants' homeland. One of the forerunners of this business was Andrea Sbarbaro, who left his native city of Genoa at the age of twelve in 1850 and by 1881 had founded a wine-making consortium called the Italian Swiss Colony, which has continued to produce fine wines for more than a century, first under its original ownership and later in the hands of another successful wine-making family, the Petris. Many others followed Sbarbaro's example, including the Spivalo family, brothers Pietro and Giuseppe Simi, Giovanni Foppiano, Vittorio Sattui, and Samuele Sebastiani.

Today, more than a hundred wineries in California are run by people of Italian descent, but the two most successful are by far the Gallo and Mondavi families.

The Gallo story is a fairly common one in the history of Italian Americans during the early decades of the twentieth century. With little to invest and nothing to lose, the Gallos were able to build a strong, successful company. The E&J Gallo Winery was founded in 1933 by Ernest and Julio Gallo, two young brothers who set up their business using their entire life savings, which amounted to less than six thousand dollars. They had neither prior experience nor any practical knowledge of wine production, and they purchased all their machinery on credit. At that time, most wine was still sent in bulk from the manufacturer to outside bottling companies. The Gallos instituted the brilliant innovation of bottling and labeling the wine directly at their own plant.

The company's success grew until, in 1972, the E&J Gallo Winery sold a total of sixteen million cases, thus becoming the largest-selling label in the United States. In 1998 the company had sales of $1.5 billion, an incredible sum in the wine sector. Today it is still a family business, run by Julio Gallo's grandchildren, Gina and Matt Gallo, wine maker and grower respectively. It has more than 3,500 employees throughout the world and exports its products to eighty-six foreign countries.

The same passion and dedication for producing fine wine is shared by the Mondavi family. Robert Mondavi and his eldest son, R. Michael Mondavi, founded the Robert Mondavi Winery in 1966. Today the company has grown to international proportions and has embarked on various joint ventures with important figures in oenology such as Baron Philippe de Rothschild.

This success story has humble beginnings as well, beginning in the early twentieth century when Robert's parents, Cesare and Rosa Mondavi, immigrated to Virginia from the Marche region of Italy. Robert's father provided a service much in demand on the West Coast: organizing shipments of fruit—grapes in particular. He fell in love with California, moved there with his family, and began to produce wine.

At first Cesare only produced enough for personal consumption, but later, as his yield grew, he began to sell it. Today his son's company has annual sales of $350 million, is listed on the stock exchange, and exports its products to ninety countries worldwide. The winery is still run by the Mondavi family; its founder, Robert, today an octogenarian, continues to be very active in the wine's promotion.

A similar success story is that of John F. Mariani, Jr., chairman and chief executive officer of Banfi Vintners, a New York firm started by his father in 1919. Especially known for importing to the United States exceptionally successful Italian and Chilean wines, Banfi Vintners has become the undisputed number one in the business. The Marianis are to be credited for their tireless efforts in the United States to promote Italian wines such as Riunite and other more elaborate, high-quality wines such as Chianti from the Cecchi family of Tuscany and Barolo from the Borgogno winery in Piedmont. Banfi also owns large vineyards in some of Italy's most renowned wine-making regions, where the company produces its own labels such as Castello Banfi di Montalcino (Tuscany), Vini Banfi Piemonte of Strevi and Principessa Gavia of Gavi (both in Piedmont).

THE FOOD INDUSTRY

The Italian presence in the United States has been beneficial not only to the wine industry but to the entire food sector. Many Italian Americans have been influential in this field, introducing or promoting such classic Italian staples as pasta and sauces that immediately won over the American palate.

One outstanding example of the Italian supremacy in this area is Joseph Pellegrino, founder of one of the nation's largest pasta producers, the Prince Company, with sales of $200 million a year. Another is Ettore Boiardi, better known as Chef Boyardee, the man who conceived of putting pasta and sauces in cans as early as the

Ettore Boiardi built a fortune on canned pasta products, such as this beef ravioli.

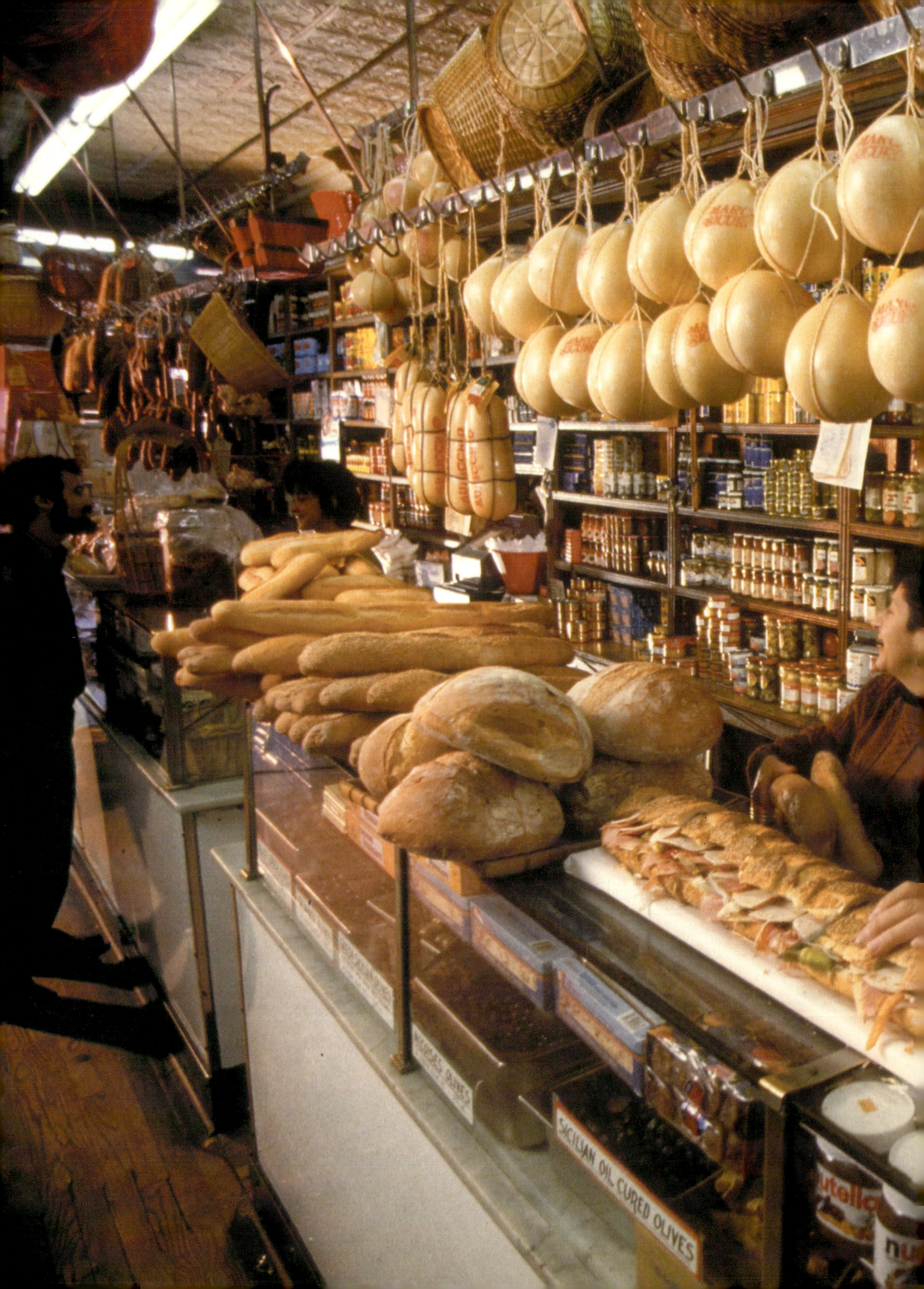
SICILIAN OIL CURED OLIVES

BUSINESS AND
ENTREPRENEURS

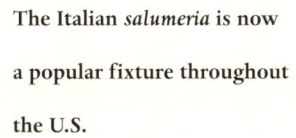

The Italian *salumeria* is now a popular fixture throughout the U.S.

1930s, foreseeing consumers' convenience-oriented approach to food decades before it became a marketing imperative.

Amedeo Obici and Mario Peruzzi were two Italian immigrants who earned their living selling peanuts on the street until they formed a partnership, founding the Planters nut company, today one of the world's largest manufacturers of toasted peanuts and other snacks.

The list of successes continues with the inventions of Mr. Coffee, the world's best-selling coffee machine, by Vince Marotta, and the founding of Blimpie and Subway sandwich shops. Blimpie, founded by Anthony Conza, has more than two thousand locations in the United States and thirteen foreign countries, while Subway, created by Fred DeLuca, has more than thirteen thousand locations in sixty-four nations worldwide.

Mario Sbarro is chairman of the board and chief executive officer of Sbarro, a chain of restaurants serving pizza and other Italian specialties, which today numbers more than nine hundred restaurants. Despite the continuing growth of his venture, Sbarro still runs his company as a "family business," supervising aspects such as quality and attentive service.

Domenico Ghirardelli and Anthony Rossi also made important contributions in the food industry; the former perfected a method of grinding chocolate that led to the invention of the chocolate bar. In the 1940s, the latter invented a pasteurization process for orange juice that allowed it to be conserved freshly squeezed, founding the Tropicana fruit juice brand, marketed today in twenty-three countries with sales of $2.5 billion a year.

Another outstanding example of achievement in the food industry is the Ferrara pastry shop in New York. This store has a very old tradition and vaunts one hundred and ten years of history. Born in 1890 as a meeting place where immigrants residing in New York's Lower East Side could finally buy typically Italian treats, the Ferrara pastry shop is named after its founder, Antonio Ferrara. He and his nephew, Alfred Lepore, watched the shop grow by leaps and bounds as the great wave of Italian immigrants started to crowd the streets of Little Italy.

Since its establishment more than a century ago, the shop has added new operations such as the production and packaging of torrone, wedding cakes, and other delectable items, thus making Ferrara a recognizable confectionery brand. Remaining faithful to its original identity as a family business, Ferrara is still run today by the Lepore family, whose contribution has made this once small shop into a New York landmark.

Finally, Italians are also in top management positions in some of the American food industry's key companies. One example is James R. Cantalupo, who serves as vice chairman of McDonald's.

Roger A. Enrico is the chairman and chief executive officer of PepsiCo, one of the world's largest and most successful consumer products companies. With $22 billion in annual revenues, PepsiCo consists of the Pepsi Cola Company, the Frito-Lay Company, and Tropicana Products. It was at Frito-Lay that Enrico started his career as a marketing manager in 1971. By 1996 he was chief executive officer and, later that year, was appointed chairman of the board. He is credited with expanding the company's beverage business, thanks to the acquisition of Tropicana (the world's number-one producer of branded juice) and with successfully taking the Pepsi Bottling Group (PBG) public on the stock market.

However, the wine and food industries, in which Italian Americans have excelled most, represent just the tip of the iceberg. Some of the most important examples of Italian Americans' enormous contributions to the U.S. economy are found in banking, finance, credit institutions, mutual funds organizations, and real estate. Other areas include the transportation industry, construction, communications, publishing, hotels, restaurants, and beauty products.

BANKING AND FINANCE

The U.S. economy owes much to an Italian American in San Francisco who, using his talent, perspicacity, and far-sightedness, revolutionized banking not only for the local Italian-American community but for the entire nation.

Amadeo Pietro Giannini was the son of Italian immigrants from Genoa who came to America during the wave of immigration at the end of the nineteenth century and eventually settled in California. He began his adventure in the world of banking when he inherited his father-in-law's position on the board of directors of a small San Francisco banking house. In 1904, he opened the first headquarters of the Bank of Italy, which over the next forty years would become one of the most important banks in America.

To fully understand the nature of the revolution instituted by Giannini, it is necessary to step back and evaluate his accomplishment in light of the economic

Amadeo P. Giannini founded the Bank of Italy in San Francisco in 1904, never imagining that it would grow into one of the world's largest financial institutions. Giannini is also known for financing the Golden Gate Bridge and California's early film industry, including Cecil B. DeMille's production of *The Ten Commandments*, and Walt Disney's *Snow White*.

and social panorama of the early twentieth century. Giannini knew that, notwithstanding the isolated successes of Italians in some areas of the American business community, the economic machine was fueled by the daily effort of hundreds of thousands of small entrepreneurs, laborers, farmers, fishermen, and artisans who supported their families and at the same time were able to save small amounts of money. These small-scale savers usually hid their savings in their homes rather than depositing them in banks, which they tended to view with suspicion. Because of the distrust they harbored for paper bills, gold was regarded as the most "realistic" currency and was kept in the house wrapped in rags and thrust under beds or in the kitchen, even inside cookie jars.

Giannini's idea was to build a bank on the savings of these small depositors, but to do this he first had to win their trust. An excellent opportunity arose following the disastrous earthquake that struck California in 1906, razing entire neighborhoods of San Francisco to the ground. The majority of workers lost their homes, jobs, and most of their possessions, and found themselves faced with the difficult task of starting over. Giannini responded by financing the rebuilding of various areas of the city and contributing to the reconstruction of the Golden Gate Bridge. Realizing that it was necessary to rekindle the hopes of thousands of people, he made signs informing the population that his bank was giving out loans and had them posted throughout the city and the surrounding communities. The loans were approved using a simple but quite unorthodox criterion; Giannini asked potential candidates to show him their hands, and if they were callused and hardened from work, the loan was theirs. With this method he earned the trust of thousands of workers who began to deposit their savings at the Bank of Italy. Giannini was always present at the bank in person, and he had the extraordinary idea of putting all his depositors' gold and money inside a large transparent safe so they could always see where their savings were and rest assured they were secure.

It was Giannini who coined the now widely used expression "money talks." From that time on, his bank thrived and the number of depositors grew daily, not only in San Francisco but eventually throughout California and in other states as well.

In 1922 he founded the Banca d'Italia e d'America in Italy, and in 1928 he changed the name of the Bank of Italy to the Bank of America after purchasing the buildings belonging to the prestigious Bank of America in New York. By 1946 the Bank of America had a total of three million depositors and half a billion dollars in deposits. Today the Bank of America, now merged with NationsBank, is one of the three largest banks in the United States and one of the biggest in the world.

Following in Giannini's footsteps is George Graziadio, founder of the Imperial Bank. Graziadio opened the first Imperial Bank in Los Angeles in 1963. In 1968 the Imperial Bancorp was formed, and today it has assets of approximately $6 billion, and capital and reserves in excess of $450 million.

SPECIAL TALENTS

One of the most significant factors in Italians' potential for professional success is their flexibility. The millions of Italians who arrived in America between 1880 and 1920 never had a problem adapting to any kind of job, work conditions, or location. Their willingness to move at a moment's notice to any city where there were employment opportunities caused them to spread throughout the nation, with a high density in the large industrial cities. Their thriftiness and zeal when it came to saving money afforded them new and better opportunities in business, and some were eventually able to purchase their employers' companies.

Examples of this extraordinary mobility and professional drive are provided by such individuals as E. B. Pasquale, a miner who struggled in his search for a better social status and respectability, left the mines, and then drifted from job to job. He went from selling toys and flags to investing and becoming one of California's first successful entrepreneurs in real estate.

An even more impressive case is that of Generoso Pope. Like many of his countrymen at the beginning of the twentieth century, Pope was a construction laborer. His enterprising character allowed him to rise through the ranks of the New York Colonial Sand & Stone Company until he became a department supervisor. Later, when the company was on the verge of bankruptcy, Pope made a deal with the owners: If he could raise the funds to pay off the company's debts, he would own of 50 percent of the company.

Pope lived up to his promise, and once he had become co-owner he expanded the company's operations and extended his control over it, finally becoming sole owner in 1927. Pope's company provided the sand and cement to build some of New York City's most famous landmarks, including Rockefeller Center and Radio City Music Hall. He became the first Italian-American millionaire in the United States and purchased the Italian-language newspaper *Il Progresso Italo-Americano* from its founder, Charles (born Carlo) Barsotti.

Today an important name in the real estate business is that of Giuseppe Cecchi, president of International Developers, Inc. (IDI), considered one of the most outstanding real estate developers in the Washington, D.C., metropolitan area. Cecchi is also known for developing the Watergate at Landmark, an award-winning condominium community of fourteen hundred units in Alexandria, Virginia.

Among the many other examples of Italian Americans who, starting with practically nothing, were able to achieve great success and build solid companies is Peter F. Secchia. A former U.S. ambassador to Italy, Secchia founded and is chairman of the board of Universal Forest Products, a company that manufactures and distributes wood products for the do-it-yourself business. Secchia is also chairman of River City Food, a chain of twenty-one restaurants and facilities for catering and banquets. In 1994 he was recognized as Michigan's outstanding self-made businessman and was honored as the state's Master Entrepreneur of the Year.

Men such as Leandro Rizzuto, Michael H. Renzulli, and the Jacuzzi family all became influential figures in the health and beauty industry. Rizzuto founded the very successful Conair Corporation in Connecticut along with his parents in 1959, with nothing but one hundred dollars and a wealth of ideas. He invented hot rollers and perfected the professional pistol-grip hair drier, an item found today in every hair salon and in many homes. Michael H. Renzulli offers another example of how beauty can become a business capable of generating more than a billion dollars in annual sales. Sally Beauty Supply, Inc., which he founded in 1972 when he bought six stores in New Orleans, now has more than two thousand shops in North America, Europe, and Japan. In the health and beauty field, both Charles Atlas (born Angelo Siciliano) and the Jacuzzi brothers were important innovators in their respective fields. In the 1920s Atlas introduced a technique of muscle development, called *isometrics,* that pits one muscle against

Clockwise from top left: Peter F. Secchia is chairman of the board of Universal Forest Products. A former U.S. Ambassador to Italy, Secchia serves on the boards of many charitable and community organizations.

Ben Cammarata, chairman and CEO of TJX Companies. Cammarata has led TJX to its current position as the leading off-price retailer of clothing and home fashions in the United States.

Andy Giancamilli is president of K-Mart Corporation and director of the National Association of Chain Drug Stores.

Roger A. Enrico is chairman and CEO of PepsiCo. PepsiCo products, include Pepsi, Frito-Lay, and Tropicana.

Right: Lee Iacocca, credited with saving the Chrysler Corporation from bankuptcy in the early 1980s, is now promoting a new venture— e-bike.com.

BUSINESS AND
ENTREPRENEURS

63

another. His technique was soon adopted by bodybuilders throughout the world. The Jacuzzis invented a jet-propulsion system for the bath, now commonly called a hydromassage or simply a Jacuzzi.

Apparel and home fashions are the specialty of Bernard (Ben) Cammarata, chairman and chief executive officer of TJX Companies, a group that includes T.J. Maxx, a company that Cammarata himself founded in 1976.

Italian Americans have also done well in the hotel business. Steven J. Belmonte, a Chicago-born career hotelier who serves as president and chief executive officer of Ramada Franchise Systems, is the longest-standing president of a national-franchise hotel chain, having served in this position since 1991. He has more than doubled the size of the Ramada chain, which today has more than a thousand hotels throughout the United States.

Another successful hotel executive lives in the "gambler's paradise" of Las Vegas. J. Terrence Lanni is the chairman of MGM Grand, the largest hotel in the United States. In March 2000 Lanni announced an exceptional merger between MGM and Mirage Resorts, another major U.S. resorts complex, which was acquired for $4.4 billion. MGM plans to build new casinos in Atlantic City as well, further expanding its influence in the industry.

Anthony A. Marnell II, on the other hand, builds the hotels of Las Vegas and designs their interiors. This Italian-American architect—owner and chairman of one of America's most powerful building companies, Marnell Corrao Associates—has built grand hotels such as the Mirage and the Excalibur. His company has provided building services for Caesars Palace, the Boyd Group, and many others. Marnell's most ambitious project to date remains the Rio Hotel & Casino, built in 1986, the world's only all-suite hotel. Marnell also serves as chairman of the board and chief executive officer of Marnell Corrao Associates. The American dream of success and wealth, however, was not achieved by everyone. For every entrepreneur who was able to achieve his dream of wealth despite

J. Terrence Lanni is chairman of the board of MGM Grand, Inc. in Las Vegas, Nevada. He also serves on the boards of many organizations, including the Keck School of Medicine, the Ronald Reagan Presidential Foundation, and the Board of Visitors of the University of California, School of Business Administration.

BUSINESS AND
ENTREPRENEURS

Michael H. Renzulli, president and CEO of Sally Beauty Supply, Inc., is shown here in one of his more than two thousand stores. He started the company in 1972 with just six stores in New Orleans and now has branches throughout North America, Europe, and Japan.

Above left: Livio DeSimone became the chairman of the board and CEO of 3M Company in 1991. DeSimone emphasizes innovation in his approach to business, and has led 3M to high levels of performance. Today 3M serves customers in approximately two hundred countries around the world.

Above right: Leonard Riggio, the founder and CEO of Barnes & Noble, is a major force among American booksellers.

Center: Robert Di Romualdo is chairman of Borders Books, which operates more than three hundred stores in the United States and abroad. He took on the position in 1994, and since that time he and his team have successfully expanded the company. In 1995 the Borders Group floated a public stock offering on the New York Stock Exchange.

Richard Grasso, left, head of the New York Stock Exchange, shares a podium with Mayor Rudolph Giuliani, right, of New York.

John F. Antioco, chairman and CEO of Blockbuster, the nation's largest supplier of home videos. He was named to the *Entertainment Weekly* list of the 101 most powerful people in the entertainment industry in 1998.

BUSINESS AND
ENTREPRENEURS

68

his humble origins during the first forty years of the twentieth century, there were hundreds of thousands of Italians who received meager wages for exhausting work on the construction of railroads and subways or in mines and factories. Many others earned no more than what they needed to live with dignity as merchants, craftsmen, farmers, or fishermen, but together they constituted a true economic force. For years in California, a very strong community of Italian fishermen, composed mostly of Ligurians and a slightly smaller number of Sicilians, maintained control of the fishing industry. The same can be said of agriculture, in which Italians as an ethnic group excelled thanks to their experience and skill in working the land.

One characteristic of Italians in America, especially those who had come from the Mezzogiorno, was their tendency to remain united through the trials of assimilation in a new society and against the openly hostile discrimination of which they, like many other ethnic groups, were often victim. The family was traditionally seen as a self-sufficient and unassailable fortress, and the same trust that Italians had in their families was given to their countrymen and townspeople, allowing them to form hardworking and productive communities that often became quite powerful.

After World War II, however, Italian Americans began to slowly abandon the insularity that had served to protect them from a larger American society they often perceived as hostile. During that same period, many Italian Americans began their rise to important positions in the business world.

It could be said that the scope of Italian accomplishments in America was directly related to their level of assmilation in American society. The first significant steps toward achieving this assimilation were taken by second- and third-generation Italian Americans, the children and grandchildren of those who had arrived in America at the turn of the century. A significant contributing factor in

BUSINESS AND ENTREPRENEURS

Above: John Paul DeJoria is Chairman and Chief Executive Officer of John Paul Mitchell Systems, which for over two decades has sold the famous Paul Mitchell hairstyling products to salons. The company now produces over ninety products and owns over one hundred trademarks.

Left: Pamela Fiori, editor-in-chief and publisher of *Town & Country* magazine.

Patricia Russo, former executive vice president and CEO of service provider networks at Lucent Technologies, with Richard Grasso of the New York Stock Exchange at a National Italian American Foundation awards ceremony.

this growing assimilation, which opened doors for new and more prestigious careers, was a higher level of education.

About 80 percent of Italian immigrants to the United States came from Southern Italy, a region traditionally reluctant to accept the importance of education for personal growth. The peasants of the Mezzogiorno were suspicious of education, seeing it as a waste of energy that should be used for the truly important activity of labor. Even children's wages were important for families' financial survival.

These immigrants brought their deeply rooted convictions with them to the United States, including the old antipathy toward formal education. Their new nation, however, was founded on different values, the foremost of which was the importance of education.

Therefore the process of Americanization necessarily included the acquisition of a certain amount of culture and knowledge. The number of Italian-American children enrolled in schools grew considerably in the second generation and continued to rise in the next. This positive attitude toward schooling was perhaps the result of a realization that education could provide more opportunities to acquire a more favorable place in society and find better jobs.

Successful men like Leonard S. Riggio have been able to capitalize on America's quest for culture, building a business empire on books. Riggio is of Sicilian heritage but was born and raised in Brooklyn. He purchased the Barnes & Noble bookstore on Fifth Avenue in New York with a loan of $1.2 million in 1971. His investment would reveal itself to be a booming business. In little more than twenty years, Barnes & Noble became an empire with more than one thousand stores in forty-nine states, forty thousand employees, and annual sales of more than $4 billion. It was recently calculated that one out of every eight books sold in the United States is purchased in a Barnes & Noble bookstore.

In the multibillion-dollar book market, there is room for another influential entrepreneur, Robert F. Di Romualdo, chairman of the Borders Group. Di Romualdo joined the company in 1989 as chief executive officer and contributed greatly to its international expansion and its successful public stock offering.

A NEW GENERATION

In the years following World War II, Italians began their rise to financial and political success. Having proved their loyalty toward their new homeland during the war and having obtained a higher level of education and assimilation in American society, they were ready to take their places at all levels of the U.S. economy.

The children of those who had fought for a more dignified life in the mines, at the construction sites, and in the textile industry finally had the opportunity to move into different, more prestigious and profitable areas of the economy. They continued their parents' tradition of inventiveness and dedication, applying Italian creativity and talent in new fields.

In the panorama of this new generation's achievements, the experience of two Italian Americans in particular shines brightly. Starting out with few means and many ideas, they developed shopping malls, further driving the U.S. economy.

In a society defined by consumerism, shopping malls were destined to become a huge success. They revolutionized shopping for the entire population of the United States. William Cafaro and Edward De Bartolo, Sr., were pioneers in this business, which is still linked to their names.

Cafaro began his journey to success when he purchased a commercial property in the 1940s, which he then resold to invest in other activities such as supermarkets, an auto dealership, and a medical center. When the fever for shopping malls broke out in the early 1950s, Cafaro had already built more than seventy structures including shopping centers, and indoor, outdoor, and regional malls covering a total of 37 million square feet. At his death in 1998, at the age of eighty-four, Cafaro left behind a legacy of more than $800 million, going down

John J. Cafaro, executive vice president of the Cafaro Company, which helped pioneer the development of shopping malls. His father, William Cafaro, began building neighborhood shopping centers in the 1940s.

George Graziadio, chairman, president, and CEO of Imperial Bank in California, plays in the Hope Classic Gold tournament. Mr. Graziadio started Imperial Bank in 1963 with $1,250,000 in capital. Today, the bank is a $7 billion asset company with offices throughout the United States. Graziadio is also one of today's top philanthropic leaders, making endowments to major universities.

Ronald L. Zarrella of General Motors, with his daughter Lilly. Zarrella is executive vice president of GM and president of GM North America.

in history as one of the richest entrepreneurs in America.

Edward De Bartolo, Sr., born and raised in Cafaro's hometown of Youngstown, Ohio, began his career as a construction worker and went on to achieve a top-level position in the construction of shopping malls and suburban office parks, reaching the height of his success in the early 1960s.

If by the mid-nineteenth century Italian Americans such as Franceso Gazzolo or brothers Enrico and Rinaldo Piaggio had already achieved great success in the real estate sector, they were no less prosperous in the automobile industry.

People like Lee (born Lido) Iacocca were able to improve their personal situations and at the same time have a profound influence on the standards of technology, aesthetics, and practicality in this sector. One of Iacocca's greatest successes was the promotion of the sporty but inexpensive Mustang, which became a best-seller in America. Iacocca started out as an engineer at the Ford Motor Company and was later appointed general manager of the Ford Division, rising up through the company's ranks until he became president in 1970.

A year after leaving Ford in 1978, Iacocca took the reins of the Chrysler Corporation. The able entrepreneur found himself at the head of a company dangerously close to bankruptcy, but during his presidency he managed to transform it completely, reaching assets of $2.4 billion in 1981. Iacocca is still remembered as the man who convinced the federal government to grant Chrysler a loan of $1.5 billion, the largest public financing ever obtained by a private American company.

Other important names in the automobile industry include John Riccardo and Eugene A. Cafiero (respectively chief executive officer and president of Chrysler prior to Iacocca's arrival), Ronald L. Zarrella, Philip Guarascio, and Lucio Noto. Zarrella has been executive vice president of General Motors and president of General Motors North America since 1998, after having been in charge of the company's North American Vehicle Sales, Service, and Marketing

Vincent J. Trosino of State Farm Insurance was appointed as vice chairman of the board in 1994 and as president in 1998. Trosino also serves on the board of trustees of the American Institute for CPCU, the Insurance Institute of America, and the Insurance Institute for Applied Ethics.

department. Within General Motors, Guarascio serves as the marketing manager and is in charge of allocating media and television advertising budgets that amount to almost $2 billion a year. Due to his influential position, he is recognized as the businessman most courted by the national media.

Along with those who make and sell automobiles, there are those who help them run. That is the area of expertise of Lucio A. Noto, who since 1993 has been president and chief executive officer of Mobil, one of the world's leading oil, gas, and petrochemical companies.

Another branch of the automobile industry is represented by insurance companies, of which the State Farm Mutual Automobile Insurance Company of Bloomington, Illinois, is one of the most notable. State Farm is also headed by an Italian American, Vincent J. Trosino, who serves as its president, vice chairman of the board, and chief operating officer.

Italian Americans can also be found in important roles in airline companies. The most influential is undoubtedly Alfred A. Checchi, member of the board of directors at Northwest Airlines, of which he was formerly co-chairman and later chairman.

LOOKING TO THE FUTURE

At the beginning of the twenty-first century, the professional situation of Italian Americans has never been better. Their presence is felt in every sector, and over the past twenty years a fairly new trend has seen a growing number of Italian Americans in finance, brokerage, and money management. This is the highest rung of the economic ladder, given that the U.S. dollar, the most powerful currency in the

Above: Angelo Mozilo, chairman and CEO of Countrywide Home Loans, receives a National Italian American Foundation Award for Humanitarian Service.

Below: Steven J. Belmonte is president and CEO of Ramada Franchise Systems. At age eighteen, he was the youngest general manager in the history of Holiday Inn.

world, is used in most international financial transactions. Businessmen of Italian origin control some of America's largest mutual fund agencies, managing the investments and pension funds of millions of Americans. This new trend corresponds to a significant increase in the number of Italian Americans who earn degrees in economics.

Looking at the economic updates on television or in any financial newspaper, one can see that many of the experts' family names are Italian. Witness Ralph Acampora, one of the most respected experts of technical market analysis. Acampora appears weekly on one of the most popular business programs on television and is highly valued as a market-trends consultant by *The Wall Street Journal* and other prestigious national and local publications.

Italian Americans are today the leaders of the three principal U.S. stock exchanges, among the most important in the world. Richard Grasso has been the first member of the New York Stock Exchange staff during its 206 years of history to steadily rise through its ranks to the chairmanship, which he attained in 1995. He had previously been appointed president and chief operating officer. Nasdaq is also run by an Italian American, Frank G. Zarb. Born of a Maltese father, Zarb has served as chairman and chief executive officer of the NASD, the parent company of Nasdaq, since 1997. Completing this formidable trio of Italian-American leaders in the stock exchange is Salvatore F. Sodano, who has been chairman and chief executive officer of the American Stock Exchange (Amex) since 1999.

Another Italian American on the front lines of the U.S. economy is Carl Pascarella, president and chief executive officer of Visa, the credit institution that issues the largest number of cards in the world. He has been with Visa since 1993, and today heads a credit empire with more than 630 million cards

Above: Robert A. Georgine, president, chairman and CEO of Union Labor Life Insurance Co. in Washington, D.C.

Below: Lawrence Auriana, the director of Kaufmann Funds.

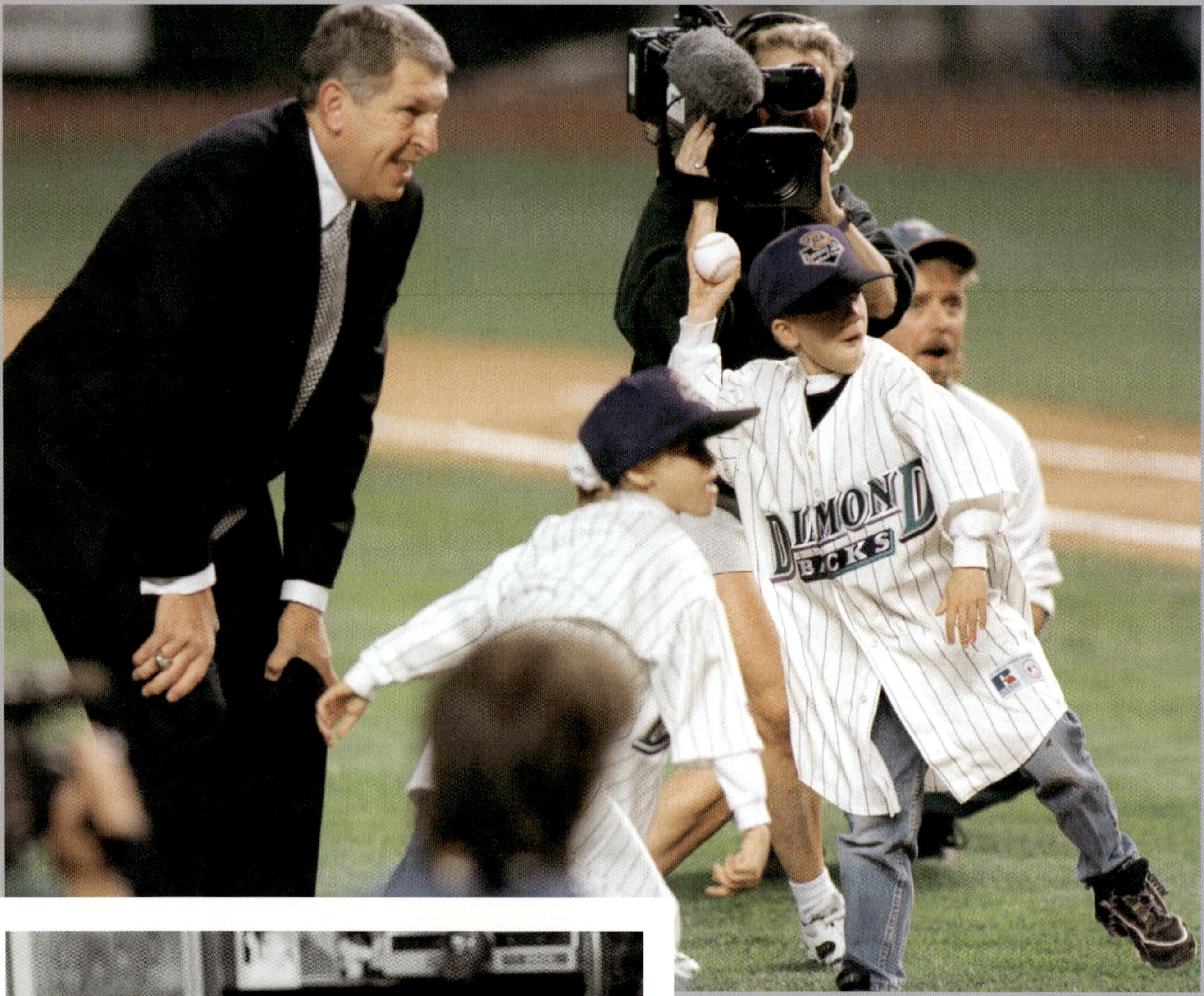

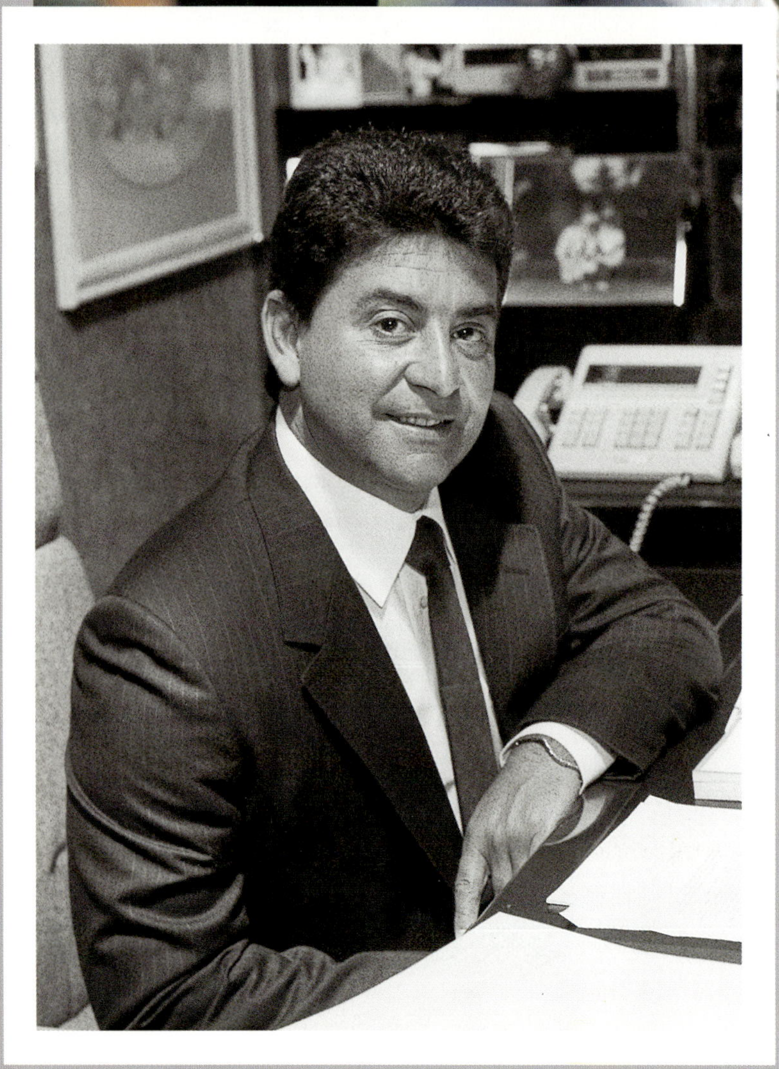

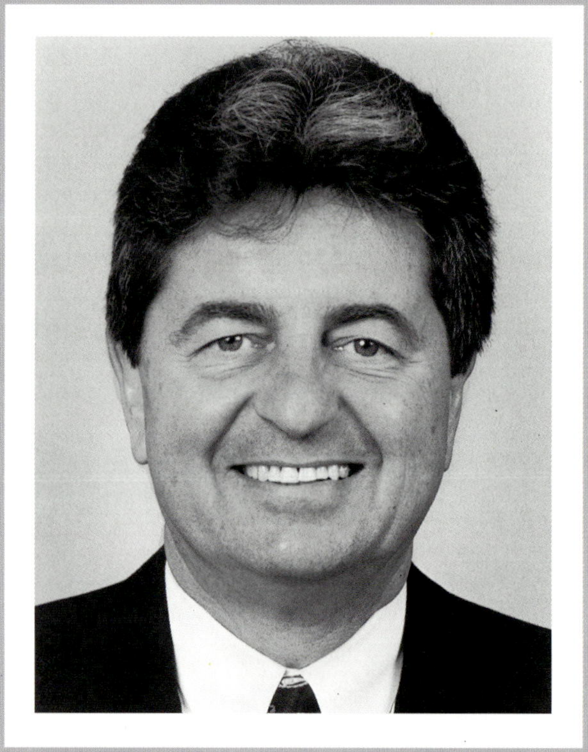

Above: Jerry Colangelo, chairman and CEO of the Phoenix Suns, supports a different team. He became the Suns' general manager in 1968 at age twenty-eight, making him the youngest general manager in sports. He is one of the top sports executives and a community leader as well, serving on the boards of many distinguished museums, foundations, and charities in the Phoenix area.

Left, below: Edward De Bartolo, Jr., is the son of an Italian-American business pioneer and owner of the San Francisco Forty-niners. His father rose from being a construction worker to owning the largest real estate company in the nation, and helped develop the shopping mall.

Right, below: Carmen Policy is president of the Cleveland Browns football team.

accepted in fifteen million locations, including 450,000 automatic teller machines on the Visa/Plus Global ATM circuit.

Examples of the strong Italian-American presence in the money-management sector are given by the success of entrepreneurs such as Angelo Mozilo, Mario J. Gabelli, Lawrence Auriana, and Thomas Marsico.

Angelo Mozilo is the classic example of a self-made man. His family, made up of both Sicilians and Neapolitans, settled in the Bronx's Little Italy in the early twentieth century. At the age of fourteen, Mozilo began to work in the mortgage industry as a messenger. Today he runs one of the largest mortgage agencies in the United States and has helped millions of Americans to buy a house. He is chairman and chief executive officer of Countrywide Home Loans and vice chairman and Chief Executive Officer of its parent company, Country-wide Credit Industries, with assets of $12 billion dollars and more than 470 branches in all fifty states.

Like Mozilo, Mario J. Gabelli was born and raised in the Bronx and is known as one of America's most successful investors. He began to invest in shares of companies such as Pepsi and ITT at the age of twelve, using the money he earned working as a caddie at a golf course. His willpower, determination, and natural flair for evaluating investments helped Gabelli purchase shares of companies with relatively low market value but great possibilities for growth.

Other figures in this sector are Lawrence Auriana, director of Kaufmann Funds, and Thomas Marsico, founder and chairman of Marsico Funds.

Over the course of the past century, Italians in America have acquired much that they were lacking in the past. Many Italian immigrants arrived in America with slender means and no education, assuming a position at the bottom of the social and economic ladders. Their ability to climb those ladders has been amazing, and their capability to keep an open mind to a new way of life while preserving a deep-rooted knowledge of their personal identity is nothing short of astonishing. During the process of Americanization, many changed their family names, others lost their knowledge of the Italian language, but none of them forgot their origins. Over the course of this long and difficult transition, the role of Italian-American women changed profoundly as well. During the last two decades of the twentieth century, women have made their presence felt in every field—politics, economics, communications, entertainment, medicine, literature, to name just a few.

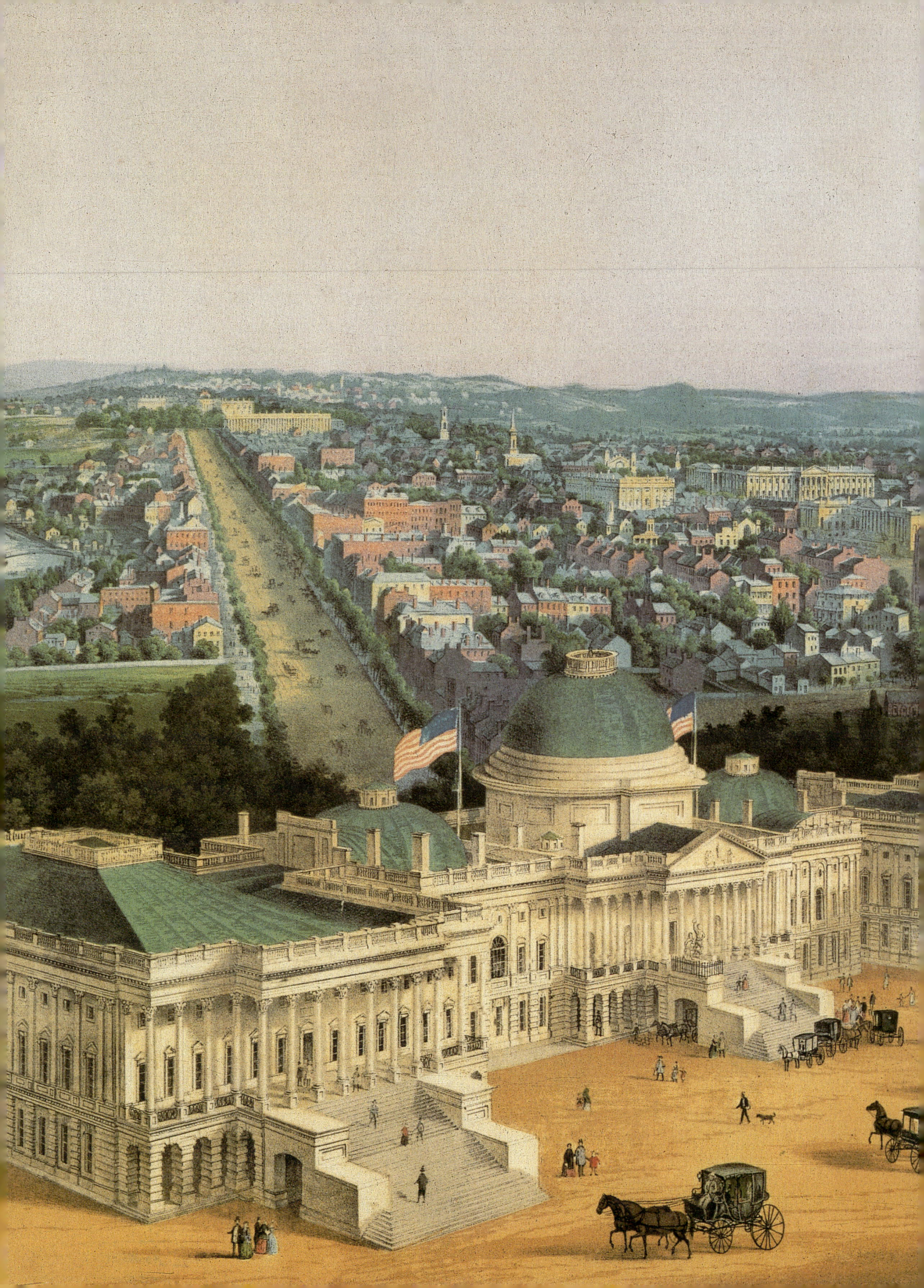

A STRONG VOICE

◆

GOVERNMENT AND PUBLIC SERVICE

The statistics regarding Italian Americans in U.S. politics at the beginning of the twenty-first century speak for themselves. Italian Americans made up only 6 percent of the total U.S. population, but there were eighty-two large cities with Italian-American mayors. Thirty-five percent of them were concentrated in New York, 31 percent in Connecticut, and another 23 percent in New Jersey. Six mayors were women.

The last U. S. Congress of the twentieth century had thirty-one members of Italian origin, including five senators and four congresswomen. Italian Americans have been part of presidential Cabinets; one serves in the U.S. Supreme Court and another, Geraldine Ferraro, was the first woman in U.S. history to ever to run for national office on a major party's ticket.

Italian-American participation has had a significant influence on U.S. politics. It has grown in direct relation to the number of people of Italian descent who live in the United States, an estimated twenty million. The number of Italian-American politicians and the prestige of their positions have also increased over the years as the Italian-American presence in the nation's sociopolitical structure has gained strength.

The first traces of Italian participation in U.S. politics date back to the eighteenth century and the friendship between the Florentine intellectual Filippo Mazzei and his neighbor Thomas Jefferson. Although he had no official role in government, Mazzei nonetheless exerted a subtle influence as statesman and humanist (see chapter 1).

View of Washington and the U.S. Capitol in the 1850s.

Francis B. Spinola, a Union general during the Civil War, was the first Italian American to serve in the U.S. House of Representatives (1887–1891). He was a Democratic representative from New York.

THE FOUNDING OF THE UNITED STATES

In 1732, an Italian, Onofrio Razzolini, had already been appointed to public office. He held the post of Armorer and Keeper of Stores in what was then the colony of Maryland. Among the signers of the Declaration of Independence were two men of Italian heritage, William Paca and Caesar Augustus Rodney. Paca was one of the first senators to sit in the Maryland legislature, and served his state as governor from 1782 until 1785. Rodney became governor of Delaware in 1778.

In 1837, John Phinizy, the son of Italian American Ferdinando Finizzi, was elected mayor of Augusta, Georgia, thus becoming the first Italian-American mayor in the history of the United States. The next one was Anthony Ghio, elected mayor of Texarkana, Texas, in 1880. Many more were to follow.

THE TWENTIETH CENTURY

Until the beginning of the twentieth century, the influence of Italian Americans in politics was marginal compared to what it is today. The Italian-American community truly came to the forefront of U.S. society only after the forty-year-long wave of immigration that began in 1880 and brought about five million Italians to the United States. As the size of the community increased, so did its need and desire to be fairly represented in local and national politics. It was toward the beginning of the twentieth century that Italian Americans began to make their presence felt strongly, exerting their influence as a substantial category of voters.

The entrance of Italian Americans into the U.S. political arena was not an easy process because their access to public life had been obstructed for decades by two important factors. First, the great majority of Italian immigrants—80 percent of whom came from poor areas of southern Italy such as Sicily, Calabria, Campania, Puglia, and Basilicata—had a significantly lower level of education than the rest of the population, a handicap compounded by their lack of familiarity with English. Second, as discussed earlier, Italians and other immigrant communities were forced to deal with strong anti-foreign sentiments that had spread throughout the country as a result of fears that immigrants would steal jobs and generally lower the standards and quality of life in the nation.

It must not have been easy for men such as Charles Bonaparte—the Italian American to whom we owe the founding of the U. S. government investigative agency that in 1935 would become the Federal Bureau of Investigation—to assume such a prestigious and powerful position at a time when numerous Italian immigrants, especially Sicilians, were still the victims of vigilante justice and lynchings. In 1906, the same year that Bonaparte was appointed the nation's attorney general by President Theodore Roosevelt, the United States paid an indemnity to Italy because of the failure of New Orleans officials to prevent the lynching of eleven Italian citizens in 1891 (see chapter 3).

Bonaparte, however, never had a problem in gaining people's trust and earning a solid reputation as a great politician and reformer. He never stooped to favoritism or false displays of friendship in order to further his career. On the contrary, he is remembered today for his honesty, persistence, and courage. When necessary, he dared to shake the U.S. political system to its very roots.

Bonaparte put pressure on the Department of Justice to investigate antitrust issues involving such powerful entities as the Standard Oil Company, the American Tobacco Company, and the Union Pacific Railroad, and this is only one example of his constant efforts as a reformer.

In 1914, Michael Rofrano was appointed deputy police commissioner of New York, providing cause for much pride and rejoicing in the city's Italian-American community. The first Italian-American detective in New York, however, was Lieutenant Joseph Petrosino, killed in Palermo in 1909 while investigating the Mafia's criminal activities. Going even further back in time, the first detective of Italian origin in the United States was Charlie Angelo Siringo, the Pinkerton undercover officer famous for his years of tracking such notorious criminals as Billy the Kid and Butch Cassidy.

Francis B. Spinola, a Democrat and former Union general in the Civil War, served in the U. S. House of Representatives from 1887 to 1891. After Spinola, the second Italian American to serve in the U. S. Congress was Anthony Caminetti, the son of immigrants who had settled in California. He became a member of Congress in 1890 after having served in his state's legislature. In 1913 Caminetti was appointed as U.S. commissioner general of immigration.

EMERGING LEADERS

In the early 1900s, Italian Americans were beginning to assume ever greater responsibilities in the national political arena. They were elected mayors and governors, as in the case of Andrew Houston Longino, who served as governor of Mississippi from 1900 to 1904, and Alfred E. Smith, whose grandfather, Alfred Emanuele Ferrara left Genoa to settle in New York at the end of the nineteenth century. Smith became the first Italian-American governor of New York in 1919. In 1928 he went down in history as the first U.S. presidential candidate of Italian descent, losing the race to Herbert Hoover.

By the end of the 1920s, other Italian Americans were joining the list of politicians elected to Congress, including Baltimore representative Vincent Palmisano, Peter Cavicchia of Newark, and Chicago representative Peter Granata. In 1938 Thomas D'Alesandro, Jr., was elected to Congress, becoming Palmisano's successor as representative of Baltimore's Little Italy, which later supported his candidacy as mayor. D'Alesandro passed on his love of politics to

4.5 Alfred E. Smith was the first Italian-American governor of New York and in 1928 was the Democratic candidate for U.S. president. He was defeated by Herbert Hoover.

his daughter, Nancy Pelosi, who was elected to the U. S. Congress in the 1980s, representing California, and to his son, Thomas D'Alesandro III, who like his father served as mayor of Baltimore.

The fiery and energetic New York City politician Vito Marcantonio served six terms in Congress (1934–36 and 1938–50). Charles Margiotti became attorney general of Pennsylvania in 1934. New York elected a mayor of Apulian origins, Fiorello La Guardia, still remembered as one of the most beloved and successful mayors in the city's political history. La Guardia, in office from 1934 to 1945, was affectionately called "the Little Flower"—a moniker that was the literal translation of the name Fiorello and also made affectionate reference to his short, stocky stature. His political career had hit its stride in 1916 when he was elected to Congress, where he fought fiercely for the rights and hopes not only of East Harlem's Little Italy (which reelected him numerous times) but of all Italian-American communities. He went to bat for causes such as the improvement of labor conditions for all ethnic groups, campaigning directly in English, Italian,

Fiorello La Guardia, the "Little Flower," was mayor of New York City from 1934 to 1945. A Republican, he was the first Italian-American mayor of that city and a strong supporter of labor unions.

Yiddish, German, and Spanish. La Guardia was also responsible for the Norris–La Guardia Act (1932), which put an end to unjust employment contracts for immigrants, recognizing their right to form unions and guaranteeing labor rules and higher wages. New York City would later commemorate La Guardia by naming one of its three airports and a college after him.

While La Guardia governed the city of New York, Angelo Rossi was serving as mayor of San Francisco. Rossi began his career with a minor position in the postal service, but his enterprising spirit and charisma made him the leading candidate in a city where the Italian community was rapidly becoming one of the most powerful.

Also in San Francisco, Generoso Pope exerted his strong yet subtle political influence. Although he was never nominated for political office, Pope's role as owner of *Il Progresso Italo-Americano*—the most widely distributed Italian-language newspaper in the country, with a daily circulation of more than 200,000 copies—made him a key figure in the political arena. The strength and influence of this publication were so great that when Franklin Roosevelt ran for president in 1940, he asked Pope to intercede in his favor with the Italian electorate.

The Italian contribution to American politics was becoming stronger and more widely felt than ever, and was destined to grow even further. In the panorama we have already described there are other illustrious names, such as that of Robert Maestri, mayor of New Orleans for ten consecutive years, Henry Selvitelli of Boston and Anne Brancato of Philadelphia, both important legislators.

World War II opened additional doors for Italian-American politicians. In light of the courage and loyalty they had shown for the United States, Italian Americans began to earn greater respect and credibility in politics in the postwar period, and as a consequence they were able to rise to more prestigious offices.

An Italian American who was particularly active in politics and also proud of his ethnic background, Michael A. Musmanno served as a judge at the Nuremberg Trials, in which the German criminals responsible for the Holocaust were judged and sentenced. Previously, Musmanno had been a defense lawyer in the trial of Sacco and Vanzetti (1921–1927), the two Italians condemned to death for a murder that many believe they did not commit. Immediately after the end of World War II, Musmanno personally conducted an investigation to confirm Hitler's death. He also fought to abolish the Coal and Iron Police, a militia whose

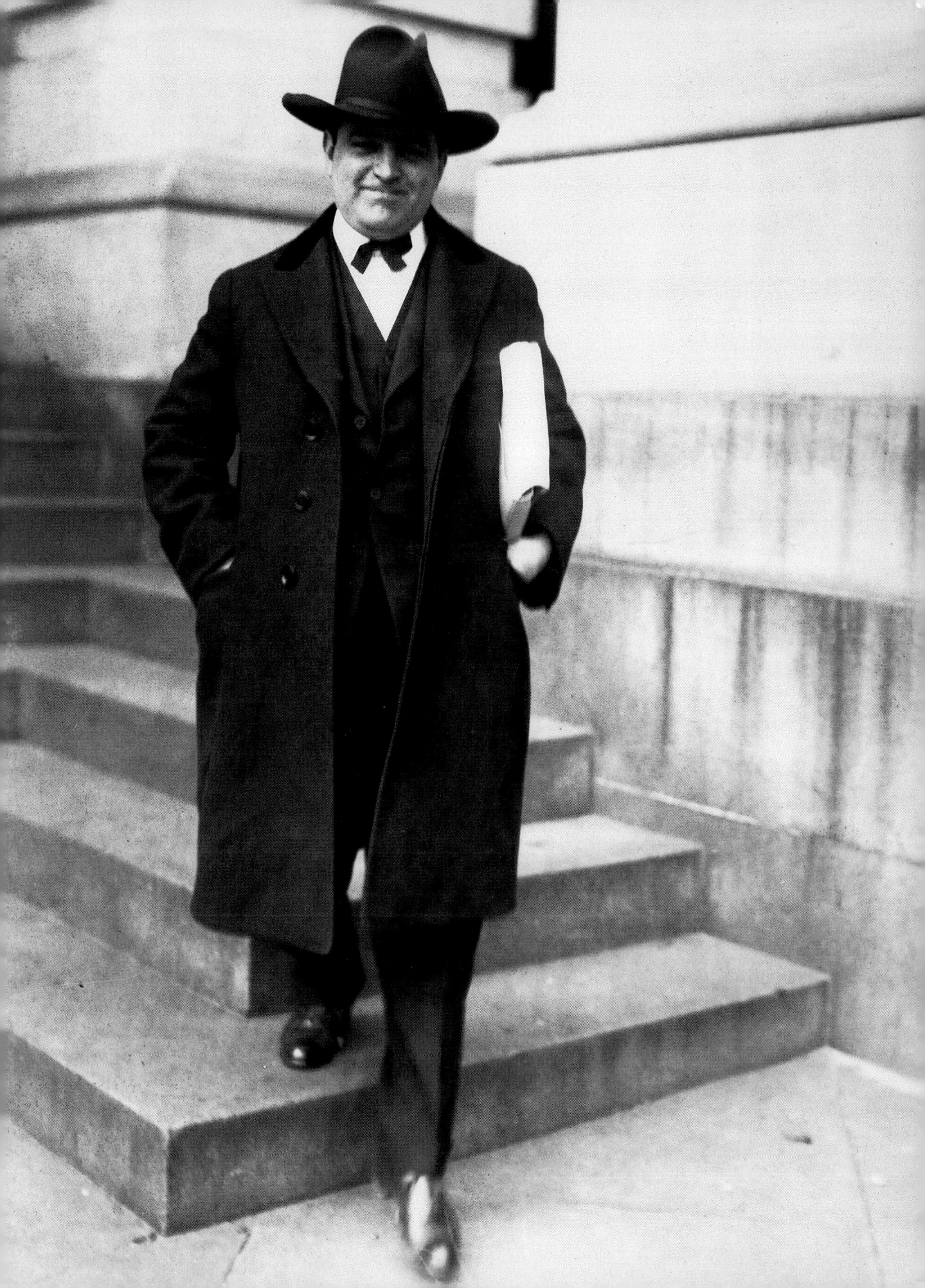

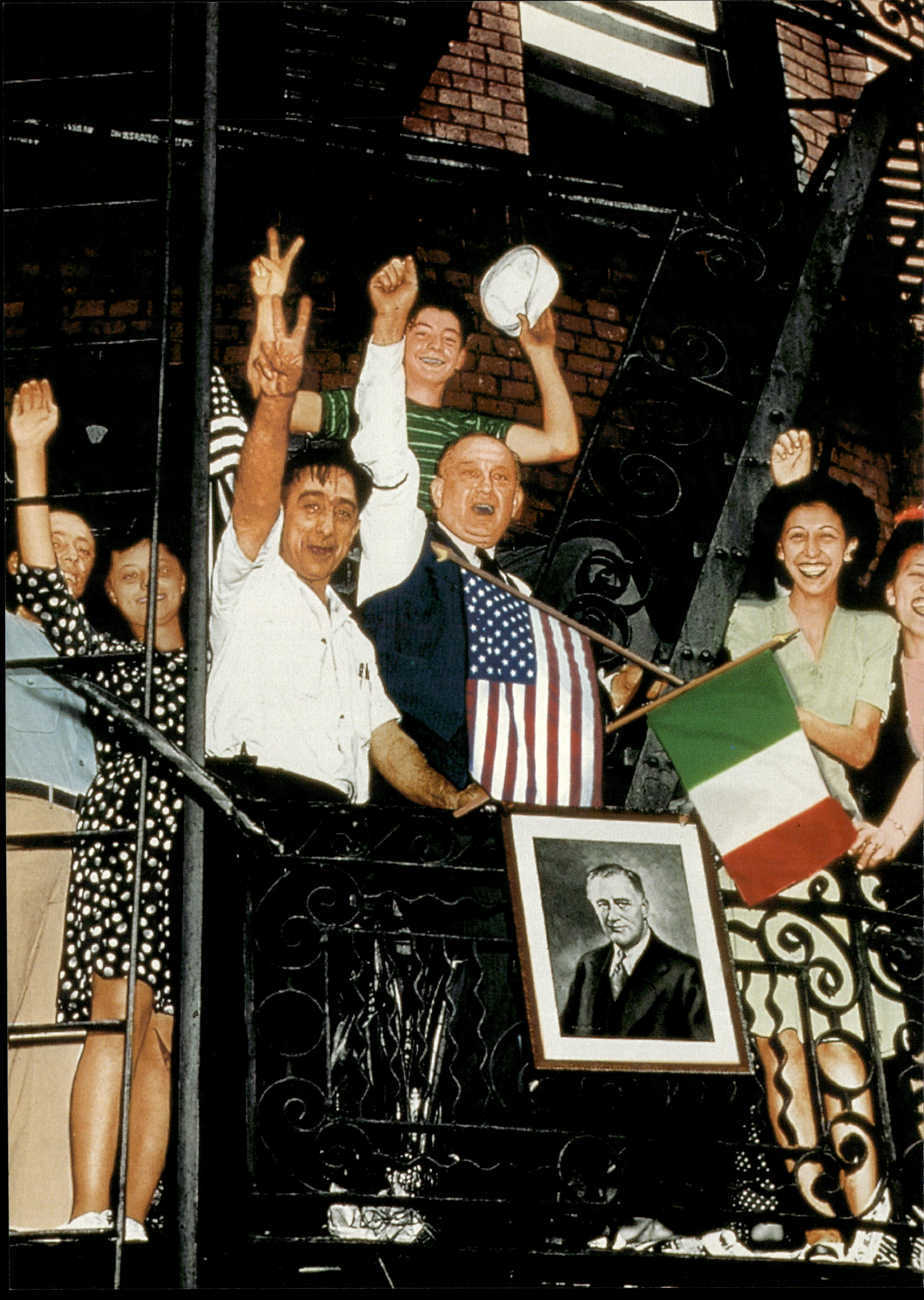

members were hired by American mine owners to intimidate workers and discourage strikes. A great admirer of Christopher Columbus, who was the subject of one of his books, *Columbus Was First,* Musmanno, coincidentally, died on Columbus Day in 1968.

Congressman Peter Rodino, elected in 1948, was another admirer of Columbus. In 1973 Rodino's efforts were key in declaring Columbus Day a national holiday. Rodino was also chairman of the House Judiciary Committee and led the committee's recommendation to impeach President Richard Nixon following the Watergate scandal in 1974. During what many consider one of the most appalling episodes in the history of the United States, the chief judge of the district in which two of Nixon's closest collaborators were prosecuted was an Italian American, John Joseph Sirica. *Time* magazine proclaimed Sirica "Man of the Year" in 1973 for his professional merits, honesty, and courage.

In 1950, John Orlando Pastore became the first Italian American to be elected to the U.S. Senate, where he remained until 1976. His career was distinguished by important duties; he became a Rhode Island assemblyman in 1934, and took office as that state's governor in 1945. In a political career that lasted more than fifty years, Pastore never lost an election.

The same record was held by Anthony J. Celebrezze, elected the first Italian-American mayor of Cleveland, Ohio, in 1953, at a time when Cleveland was the eighth largest city in the United States. Celebrezze served five consecutive terms as mayor, and in the last election received 70 percent of all votes. The son of immigrants from Potenza, in the Basilicata region, Celebrezze holds an impressive place in history as the first non-native to ever be appointed to the Cabinet. In 1962 John F. Kennedy named Celebrezze secretary of the Department of Health, Education, and Welfare (today's Department of Health and Human Services).

Another historical first occurred in 1950, further demonstrating how much ground Italians had won in the nation's political panorama, when the race for mayor of New York was held entirely among Italian Americans: Edward Corsi for the Republicans, Vincent Impellitteri for the Experience Party, and Ferdinand Pecora for the Democrats. Impellitteri won by a large margin of votes, becoming the first New York mayor born in a foreign country (he was born in Sicily) and remaining in office until 1954. Then in 1958, Christopher Del Sesto became Rhode Island's first Republican governor of Italian origin.

An Italian-American family celebrates the end of World War II in New York's Little Italy.

A REMARKABLE PRESENCE

By the early 1970s the Italian-American political presence had grown astonishingly, and over the next two decades the quantity and quality of their positions were destined to reach unprecedented heights. While two other Italian Americans, Frank Rizzo and Richard Caligiuri, were taking their places as the mayors of Philadelphia and Pittsburgh respectively, an Italian-American woman named Ella Tambussi Grasso was preparing for her rise in politics.

Grasso climbed every rung of the political hierarchy: She served as a member of the Connecticut House of Representatives from 1953 to 1957, as Connecticut secretary of state from 1958 to 1970, as a U.S. congresswoman from 1971 to 1974, and as the governor of Connecticut from 1975 to 1980. Along with being the first woman ever elected governor in her own right, Grasso is also remembered as a determined and resolute woman possessed of a strong maternal feeling and proud of her Italian origins. She fought for an open government that would allow people to have free access to and use of public records.

Always attuned to the needs and daily struggles of the working class, she gave a brilliant example of economizing when she refused a pay raise of $7,000, sending it back to the state treasury. Armed with a liberal spirit and a willingness to help others, she is still remembered by many in Connecticut for the time when, during a terrible blizzard in the winter of 1978, she spent long days in the state armory, where she tirelessly managed emergency operations and encouraged citizens during several television appearances. The only enemy able to get the best of this "human hurricane" was cancer, which took her life in 1981.

Ella Grasso's example heralded women's arrival in positions of power. At the beginning of the twentieth century, Italian-American women's first priority was the home and the family, but now the next generation of women was becoming interested in government. And these women aimed very high, as demonstrated by the career of Geraldine Ferraro. In an unprecedented event in the history of the United States, a woman—and an Italian American, no less—was nominated as a vice presidential candidate in 1984.

Whereas Ferraro came close to the White House as a vice presidential candidate, Leon Panetta was the first Italian American to have his office "twenty steps from the Oval Office and the most influential political leader in the world," to paraphrase President Bill Clinton.

Thirty years into his political career, Panetta was appointed as White House chief of staff by Clinton in 1994 and remained in that post until 1997. After having served as special assistant of the secretary of Health, Education, and Welfare, director of the U.S. Office for Civil Rights, and executive assistant to the mayor of New York, Panetta was elected to Congress in 1976 as a representative from California, where he remained for seventeen years. Before becoming White House chief of staff, Panetta had served as White House director of the Office of Management and Budget, working closely with Clinton on plans to reduce the deficit.

Cabinet members Benjamin Civetti, Joseph Califano, Frank C. Carlucci, and John A. Volpe have also held very important positions. Civetti was a U.S.

Geraldine Ferraro, of Italian descent, was the first American woman to run for a national office with a major party in the United States. In 1984 she was nominated for vice president and ran with presidential candidate Walter Mondale on the Democratic ticket. She served in the U.S. Congress from 1979 to 1985.

John Podesta served as White House chief of staff under President Bill Clinton.

attorney general; Califano was secretary of Health, Education, and Welfare during the Carter administration; Carlucci served as secretary of defense during the Reagan administration. Volpe served as governor of Massachusetts from 1961 to 1963 and again from 1965 to 1969. He was secretary of transportation from 1969 until 1973 and was U.S. ambassador to Italy from 1973 to 1977.

At the helm of the Internal Revenue Service (IRS) is another Italian American, Charles O. Rossotti. Rossotti has been commissioner of internal revenue since 1997, running a branch of the Department of Treasury that boasts 102,000 employees and a $7.8 billion budget. Rossotti's contribution to the IRS has been a new openness toward taxpayers in the form of stronger customer service and modernization of the organization through an increased use of technology. Collecting $1.5 trillion in taxes per year is not an easy task, and it has been estimated that the IRS has to deal with 100 million taxpayers by phone every year and another six million directly at its offices throughout the United States.

The Cabinet of President Theodore Roosevelt, including Charles J. Bonaparte, third from right, who in 1908 founded the agency that would become the FBI. Bonaparte was the first Italian American appointed to a cabinet position, serving as secretary of the navy and then as U.S. attorney general during the Roosevelt administration.

The swearing-in of Congressman Rick Lazio (R., New York) in 1999. In 2000, Lazio was a candidate for senator in New York State. His opponent was Hillary Rodham Clinton.

Above: FBI Director Louis J. Freeh is also of Italian descent. His mother's name was Bernice Chianciola.

Center: Constance Morella is a Republican congresswoman from Maryland.

Below: Leon Panetta, a former U.S. congressman from California, was the first Italian American to serve as White House chief of staff. He was appointed in 1994 by Bill Clinton and served until 1997.

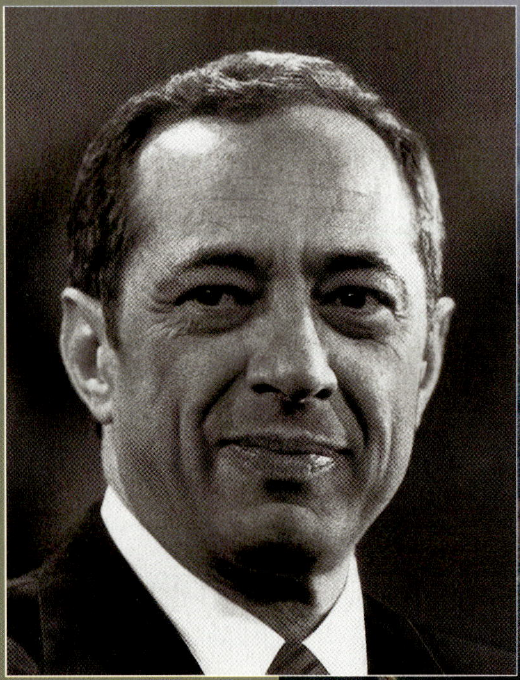

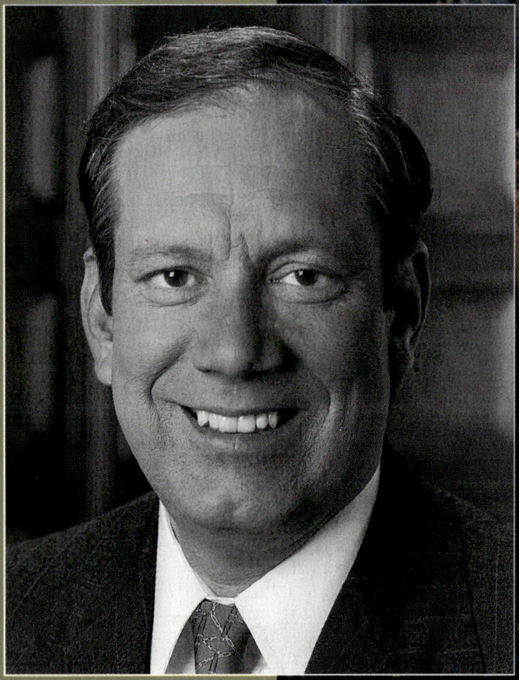

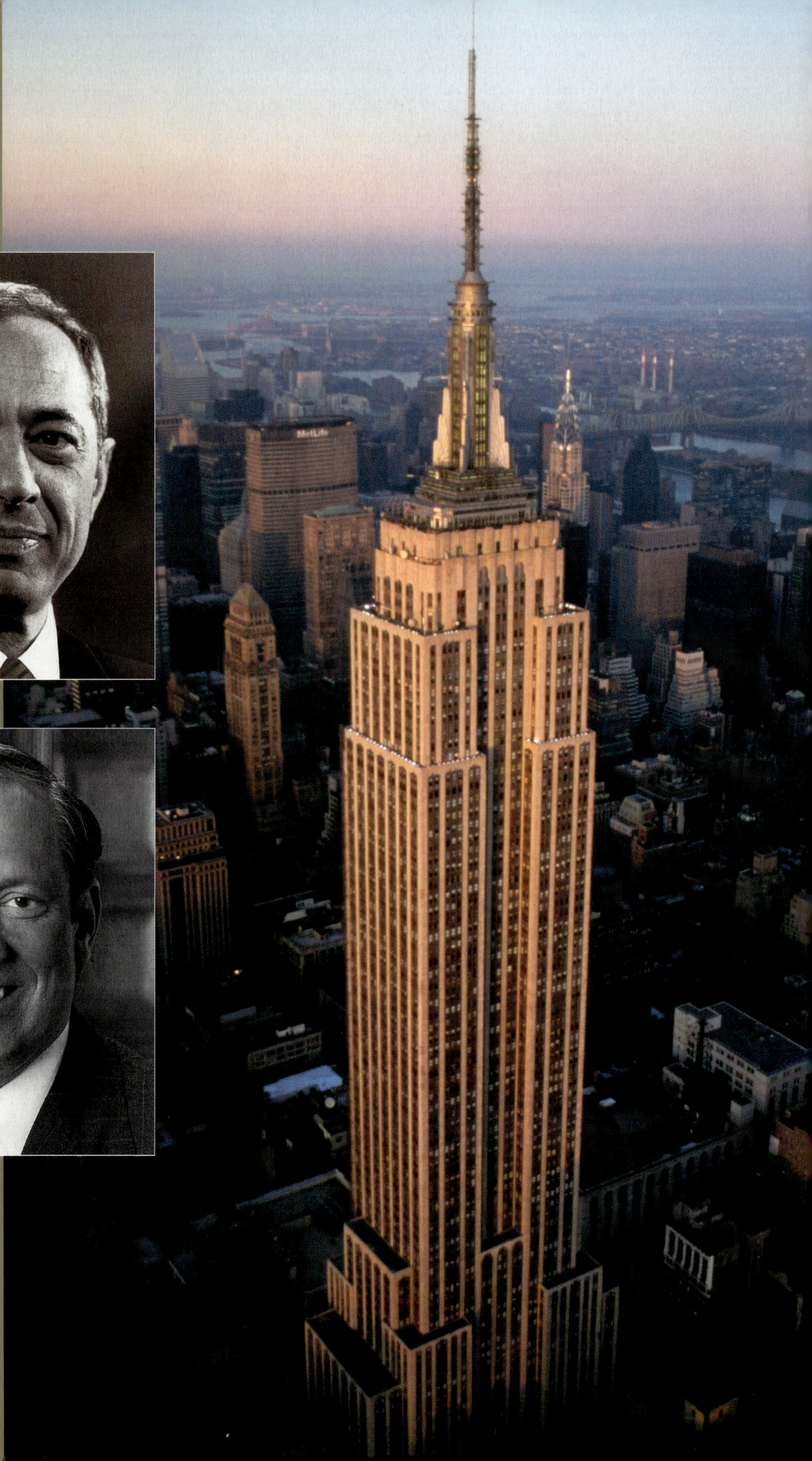
MetLife

TODAY'S LEADERS

Charles Bonaparte founded the Federal Bureau of Investigation, and almost ninety years later another Italian American became its director in 1993. Despite his misleading family name, Louis J. Freeh is Italian American; his mother, Bernice Chianciola, was originally from the Abruzzi region of Italy. Freeh was an FBI agent from 1975 to 1981, stationed in New York and at the bureau headquarters in Washington, D.C. He then went to work in the U.S. Attorney's Office for the Southern District of New York, first as deputy U.S. attorney and later as associate U.S. attorney. During this period, Freeh was the lead prosecutor in the "Pizza Connection" case, a long and complicated investigation into illegal drug trafficking from Sicily to the United States that involved pizza parlors as a cover. In 1987 another important case in the history of the fight against organized crime was the trial of Mafia boss John Gotti, which lasted more than six months and was conducted by an Italian-American U.S. district attorney, Diane Giacolone.

Returning to traditional politics, we find another illustrious Italian American who for at least a decade was considered a potential U.S. presidential candidate: Mario Cuomo, former governor of the state of New York. He was elected governor in 1982 and re-elected in 1986 with 64 percent of the votes, the largest margin in the history of the state. He is considered a skilled and constructive politician, who during his administration dealt with important issues such as safety (he introduced the seat belt law), justice, education, environmental protection, children's health, and civil rights. During his twelve-year governorship (1982–1994), Cuomo invested more than $50 billion in the growth of the private business sector, creating jobs for half a million people.

Cuomo was defeated by another politician of Italian descent, George E. Pataki, whose mother is Italian American. Pataki was a lawyer who began his career as a private legal consultant in 1970. Before becoming governor, he had been mayor of Peekskill, New York, from 1981 to 1984, a member of the New York State Assembly from 1984 to 1992 and of the New York State Senate from 1992 to 1994.

At the beginning of the new millennium, New York is the world's most powerful metropolis—a crossroads of cultures, ethnicities, and traditions—guided by an Italian American mayor, Rudolph W. Giuliani, elected in 1993 and reelected in 1997.

Above: Mario Cuomo was first elected governor of New York in 1982. He won his 1986 reelection with 64 percent of the vote, the largest margin in the state's history. He supported important programs in children's health care, human rights, housing, and the environment.

Below: New York Governor George Pataki. His mother's family is from Italy.

U.S. Supreme Court Justice Antonin Scalia, the son of Sicilian immigrants, is the first Italian American to serve on the Supreme Court. He was appointed in 1986 by Ronald Reagan.

Giuliani has conducted a firm and successful anticrime campaign in New York, achieving a 41 percent decrease in the number of all crimes committed and a 48 percent decrease in the number of murders during his first term alone. Giuliani's policies have transformed New York into a tranquil, livable city by exacting harsh punishment even for such minor crimes as car theft, black-market commerce on the street, and vandalism, thus discouraging more serious crimes. New York was named the safest city in the United States in an FBI crime report written at the end of the 1990s.

The last two decades of the twentieth century have seen an intense participation of Italian Americans at every level of public service. Among the many U.S. mayors of Italian origins is the first Italian American mayor of Boston, Thomas Menino, elected in 1993. On the list of Italian Americans who have served the U.S. Senate, two other capable politicians are worth mentioning: Dennis DeConcini of Arizona and Pete Domenici of New Mexico. DeConcini was described by the *New York Times* as "one of the most intelligent, intense and hardworking members of the Senate" (May 1995). In 1972 Domenici became the first Republican in thirty-eight years to be elected to the U.S. Senate from New

Mexico. With his reelection in 1996, Domenici became the first New Mexican elected to serve five full six-year terms in the Senate, quite an accomplishment considering that the American Southwest is an area with a low density of Italian Americans compared to other states. The first Italian American to be elected to the U. S. Senate from New York, on the other hand, was Alphonse D'Amato, who was strongly supported by his native Nassau County. In the House of Representatives, Italian Americans have a growing presence. By the year 2000, 26 were serving, and a former U.S. congressman, Frank J. Guarini now leads the National Italian American Foundation. Guarini, a seven-term congressman from New Jersey, was the first member ever appointed to the House's powerful Ways and Means Committee on his first day in office.

Further proof of the level of power that Italian Americans have reached was the naming of Antonin Scalia as a justice of the United States Supreme Court in 1986. Scalia is the first and only Italian American to hold this title, thus reaching the highest national position ever attained by an individual of Italian descent in the history of the United States. Before his nomination to the Supreme Court by President Ronald Reagan, Scalia held various positions, including that of general counsel to the president's Office of Telecommunication Policy and assistant attorney general in the Office of Legal Counsel in the U.S. Department of Justice. Scalia has always supported a "textualist" approach to the U. S. Constitution. He firmly believes in applying the laws in the original linguistic terms in which they were conceived, avoiding the current tendency to search for new interpretations and alternative meanings.

While it would be a daunting task for us to mention all the worthy men and women who have worked in federal, state, and local governments, in public service and law enforcement, their considerable numbers indicate that Italian Americans show a pattern of rapid growth and heightened participation in this nation's public life. They begin the new millennium with a concrete foundation built on past achievements and with the well-founded hope that someday one of them will arrive at the highest and most coveted office in the land, that of president of the United States.

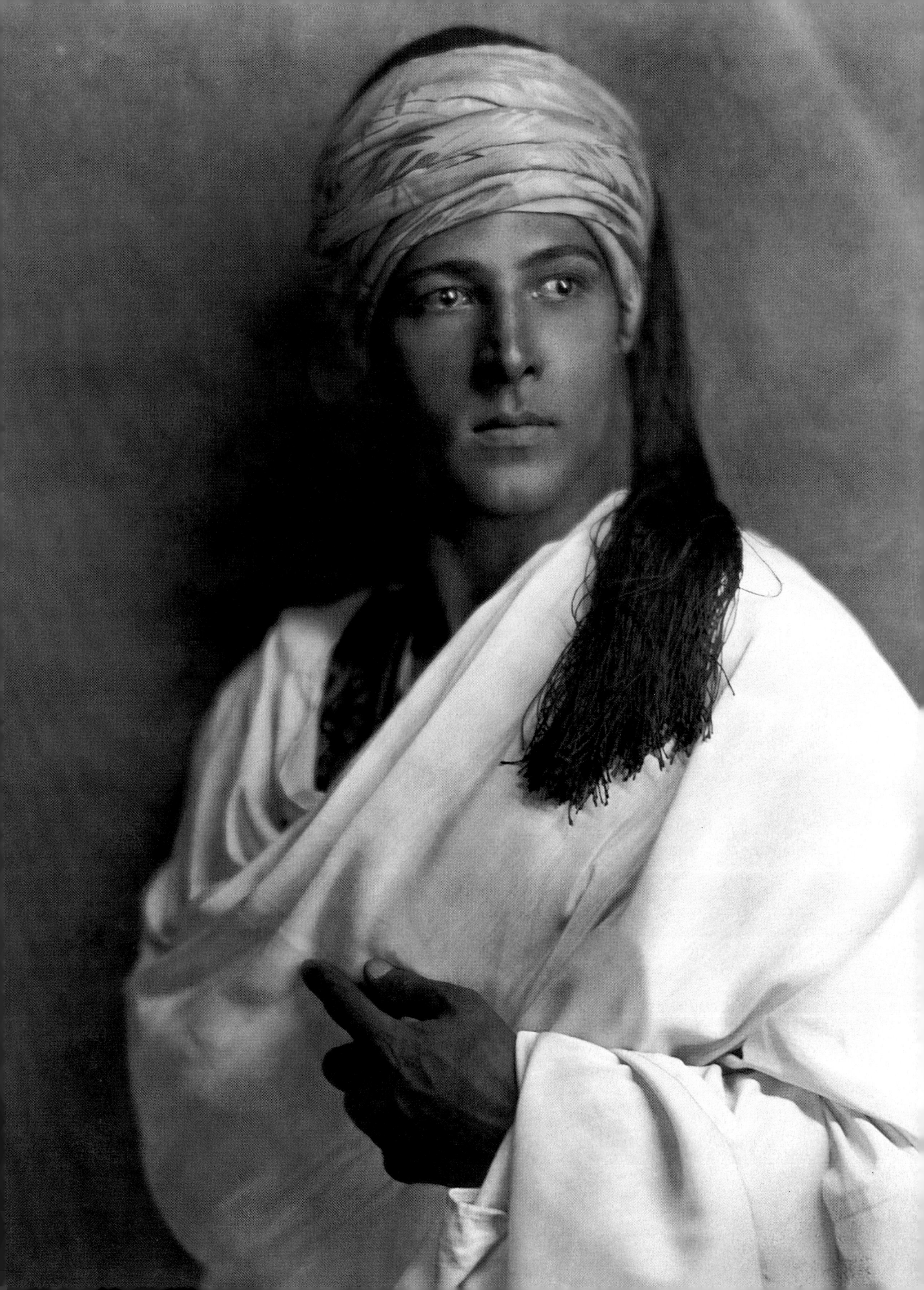

ARTS AND ENTERTAINMENT

Italy has a long history of creativity that began with Virgil and Ovid in Ancient Rome, flourished in the Middle Ages with Dante, Petrarch, Masaccio, and Fra Angelico, and reached extraordinary heights in the Renaissance with Michelangelo, Leonardo da Vinci, Raphael, and a host of other artists. For more than two thousand years, Italians have made remarkable contributions to music, art, literature, architecture, theater, and every other creative endeavor.

So it is not surprising that among the millions of immigrants who flocked to the United States from Italy there were many who brought with them the seeds of great talent and creativity. So many Italian Americans have become stars in music, cinema, and art that it would be impossible to name them all in the limited space afforded by one chapter.

Rudolph Valentino in his role in *The Sheik*. Valentino was Hollywood's first sex symbol. Born Rodolfo Guglielmi in Castellaneta, Italy, in 1895, he rose to stardom in the teens and 1920s, making eighteen movies between 1914 and 1926. He died at age thirty-one of a ruptured appendix.

OPERA

Spectacular operatic exhibitions were already being promoted in America at the beginning of the nineteenth century by Lorenzo Da Ponte, Mozart's librettist, who had collaborated with the famous composer for the operas *Cosi fan tutte, Le Nozze di Figaro,* and *Don Giovanni.* Da Ponte came to the United States in 1803 and encouraged the growth of the lyric theater across the nation, promoting many operas and especially those by Mozart.

In a short time, he had aroused the interest of such European opera singers as the famous sopranos Luisa Tetrazzini and Adelina Patti, who subsequently moved to the United States. For the Italians in America opera reminded them of

The great Enrico Caruso, one of the most renowned tenors of all time.

the country they had left behind. Since Americans were also very appreciative of opera, this form of entertainment created a cultural bridge between Italy and the United States.

By the beginning of the twentieth century, one of the most respected opera singers in the United States was the soprano Rosa Ponselle, born in Connecticut of Southern Italian immigrant parents. Her father, an amateur singer, encouraged her to pursue her talent. She sang in a church choir with her sister and also performed with her in vaudeville. Ponselle was barely out of her teens when her full, expressive voice was discovered by Giulio Gatti-Casazza, the Italian director of the Metropolitan Opera in New York. Ponselle's debut at the Met in 1918 was in Giuseppe Verdi's *La Forza del Destino,* performing with the most accomplished tenor of the time, Enrico Caruso.

Many Italians have enchanted American operagoers over the course of the twentieth century, including the soprano Licia Albanese, bass Ezio Pinza, and the legendary orchestra conductor Arturo Toscanini.

Alongside these more traditional operatic talents is the American-born Mario Lanza, who was the first to successfully blend opera and cinema. Although his rich, powerful tenor voice afforded him an operatic repertoire that included the role of Pinkerton in Puccini's *Madame Butterfly,* his fame remains tied to such Metro-Goldwyn-Mayer films as *The Toast of New Orleans* and *The Great Caruso.*

One noteworthy operatic composer of recent times is Gian Carlo Menotti, whose works include *The Telephone* (1947), *Amahl and the Night Visitors* (1951), and *The Saint of Bleecker Street* (1954), an opera set in a modern Little Italy. Menotti twice received the Pulitzer Prize and also founded the Festival of Two Worlds, held annually in Spoleto, near Perugia, and in its U.S. sister city, Charleston, South Carolina.

Another composer, John Corigliano, first came to prominence after winning the chamber music prize at Menotti's Spoleto Festival in 1964. Corigliano's opera *The Ghosts of Versailles,* commissioned by the Metropolitan Opera, premiered in 1991. Corigliano won an Academy Award in the year 2000 for his score for the film *The Red Violin.*

Composer Dominick Argento won the Pulitzer Prize for Music in 1975 for *From the Diary of Virginia Woolf,* as did David Del Tredici in 1980 with his composition *In Memory of a Summer Day.*

ARTS AND
ENTERTAINMENT

101

A dinner in honor of Giulio Gatti-Casazza and conductor Arturo Toscanini at New York's Hotel St. Regis, November 22, 1908.

Italian-born Giulio Gatti-Casazza was director of the Metropolitan Opera in New York from 1908 to 1935. He brought to the stage an amazing array of singers, including Enrico Caruso, Rosa Ponselle, and Ezio Pinza.

Opposite, Rosa Ponselle, an extraordinary talent, debuted at the Metropolitan Opera in 1918. She was the first American singer to perform there who had not received European training. She played more than twenty roles during her nineteen-year career.

ARTS AND
ENTERTAINMENT

103

The most prestigious opera house in the United States, the Metropolitan, is directed by Joseph Volpe, who began his career at the Met as a carpenter twenty-five years ago.

BALLET AND THEATER

In the history of American ballet, the French dominated for the first half of the nineteenth century. Their technique was considered the height of grace and was the primary resource of every important American dance company. The arrival of the Italians during the second half of the nineteenth century changed the American concept of dance drastically and permanently.

Dancers and teachers such as Carlo Blasis revolutionized dance with difficult and intricate techniques involving new moves, turns, pirouettes, and jumps. Americans were enchanted by the intensity and drama of these dancers, who completely ousted the French, taking their place at the forefront. For more than a century, Italian techniques, revered by audiences and critics, were the most frequently taught, representing the highest standard of movement and bodily expression. Even during the second half of the twentieth century, when the Russians redefined ballet throughout the world, Italian dancers continued as examples of refinement, technique, and fullness of expression.

Among the numerous Italian and Italian-American ballet dancers who have graced American stages over the decades are Rosina Galli, Maria Gambarelli, Gisella Caccialanza, Fred Danieli, and Enrico Cecchetti. Cecchetti is considered by many to have been the most influential dance teacher of all time. Many ballet dancers today are still trained according to the Cecchetti Method.

Edward Villella, by far one of the most famous male dancers during the 1960s and 1970s, brought to the stage a synthesis of virility and gracefulness, thus becoming a model for many future dancers. With the goal of promoting knowledge and awareness of dance among those who did not frequent the theater, Villella danced many times on television programs, and consequently achieved a high level of public recognition.

Dancers such as Kay Mazzo, Eleanor D'Antuono, and Gerald Arpino guaranteed the continuing popularity and success of their art, and the contributions of many Italian Americans behind the scenes, from choreographers to the artistic directors of dance companies, were fundamental as well.

THE QUEEN GREETS MARIO LANZA...

Mario Lanza, a gifted tenor who rose to fame in the 1940s and 1950s, became the first vocalist to sell 2.5 million albums. Born Alfred Cocozza in Philadelphia in 1921, he took his mother's name as his stage name. Lanza had a brief Hollywood career before dying prematurely at age thirty-eight.

MUSICAL THEATER

Many Italian Americans played important roles behind the scenes, achieving memorable accomplishments in the world of dance, theater, and musicals. Not everyone knows, for instance, that two of the most famous musicals in the modern history of Broadway, *A Chorus Line* and *West Side Story,* were choreographed by Italian Americans. *A Chorus Line* was conceived, written, directed, and choreographed by Michael Bennett. *West Side Story* was choreographed by Jerome Robbins, whose talented assistant, Peter Gennaro, originated the Latin choreography that pervades the entire musical and its cinematic rendition. Gennaro went on to help create the choreography of such other successful Broadway musicals as *Fiorello!* and *Annie.*

For Italian immigrants, the theater was a very important part of their lives. The majority of immigrants held a separatist attitude toward the new American

Above: Arturo Toscanini conducting.

Right: The extraordinary dancer Rosina Galli, performing in 1915.

society, which they saw as incompatible from the standpoint of language, customs, and mentality. After hard days spent at work, nostalgic for their homeland and its familiar ways, the immigrants regarded the theater as a refuge and an escape from their worries. At the theater they socialized, fleeing the sense of isolation they often suffered. Although many of them were not familiar with opera, they responded enthusiastically to theatrical productions, especially those with comic themes.

In New York, where Italian theater in the United States was born and thrived, Italians particularly revered actors who performed in vaudeville, caricatures, and sketches. These actors impersonated characters from real life, imitating their accents and wearing funny costumes, mixing English with Italian and regional dialects to create a curious theatrical Babel.

One of the funniest and most unforgettable actors of the early twentieth century was Eduardo Migliaccio, called Farfariello (Little Butterfly) for his irresistible impersonation of the idling, womanizing immigrant. During his long and successful career, he created a rich collection of characters, including a chimney sweep, a fireman, an opera singer, a gangster, an Irish policeman, and even a nun.

Light comedy was the most popular and easily enjoyable form of entertainment, but in the first two decades of the twentieth century, Italian theater gained new depth and maturity, introducing literary, political, and social elements. Antonio Maiori, a theater actor and director, was the first to present Shakespeare to the Italian-American public, and made it more comprehensible to his audience by translating it into Italian and sometimes into dialect. Thus theater gained a new importance as an educational tool in Italian-American society.

Other playwrights, such as Salvatore Abbamonte and Riccardo Cordiferro, created pieces for the theater based on real-life situations, highlighting the difficulties immigrants had with their jobs and their American neighbors. Their plays

ARTS AND
ENTERTAINMENT

107

told of exploitation, of the hostility of *padroni* (Italian employment brokers), of fatigue and alienation.

However, since Italian theater in America relied on the presence of immigrants, who constituted the majority of its audience, it lost its glow when immigration began to slow after the 1920s. Moreover, as people of Italian origin acquired greater fluency in English and gradually began to assimilate into American society, they became interested in other popular forms of entertainment such as radio and cinema.

Eventually the immigrant Italian-American theater fell to a position of secondary importance. After the 1950s, one could say that this theater disappeared completely, with the exception of a few artists who still promote the Italian spirit. One of these artists is Mario Fratti, who continues to write remarkable plays in both Italian and English.

THE SILVER SCREEN

In Italian-American theater the actors' fame was confined to a limited ethnic audience, but in the world of cinema Italian Americans have won affection and popularity throughout the United States and the world. The most obvious examples are actors, but the laurels of success also adorn numerous directors, producers, costume designers, and every type of professional in the world of filmmaking.

As early as the 1920s, when Rudolph Valentino enchanted audiences in *The Sheik*, it was clear that Italians and Italian Americans had much to offer American cinema, and not only as actors. Ideas and subjects stemming from Italy's culture and way of life inspired many directors to make films about the country, its immigrants, and other related themes. This could partly explain the enormous presence and influence that Italian culture has had on the American psyche.

Cinema, more than any other art form, is responsible for the creation and growth of stereotypes of Italian Americans: gangsters, jealous lovers, boxers, and pious mothers are the core characters of a particular Italian-American culture that thrives in the American imagination largely because of Hollywood. Many of these stereotypes, such as the enormously negative one of the mafioso, typify an entire genre of filmmaking and have continued to survive in television shows and advertising through the beginning of the twenty-first century.

Some Italian Americans like Mario Puzo and David Chase, have exploited their own heritage to succeed in the world of entertainment, but others like Frank Capra, chose a completely different artistic direction. Capra, one of the most popular film directors of the thirties and forties, achieved success with movies that told of the American dream, such as *It's a Wonderful Life, American Madness,* and the highly acclaimed *It Happened One Night,* winner of five Academy Awards.

The first two decades of the twentieth century also saw the presence of Italian-American actors on the silver screen, even before the actor Rudolph Valentino burst on the scene. The first film version of *Cinderella* (1911), for example, saw in the title role Mabel Talliaferro, who enjoyed fame along with her sister, Edith Talliaferro, also an actress. Twenty-five years later, Adriana Caselotti provided the voice of the heroine in the 1937 Walt Disney animated version of *Snow White,* the first full-length cartoon in history.

By the 1940s and 1950s Italian-American actors began appearing in important films, often playing leading roles in prestigious productions: Don Ameche (born

This poster advertises director Frank Capra's classic motion picture *It's a Wonderful Life.* Capra came to the United States from Sicily at age six. He won three Academy Awards for best director, and remains today a legend in Hollywood. Capra died in 1991 at age 94.

Mira Sorvino won an Academy Award for her role in Woody Allen's *Mighty Aphrodite*. Her father, Paul Sorvino, is also a respected actor.

Dominic Felix Amici) starred in Ernst Lubitsch's *Heaven Can Wait.* (1943); Ernest Borgnine (born Ermes Elforon Borgnino) won an Academy Award for Best Actor in 1955 for his performance in the title role of *Marty.* The careers of Robert and Alan Alda, Tony Franciosa, Ben Gazzara, Vincent Gardenia, and Paul Sorvino, to mention only a few of the most representative names, have been remarkably successful.

Italian-American women also garnered their share of praise in the world of cinema, as is proved by the success of such actresses as Anne Bancroft, born Anne Marie Louise Italiano, who is remembered best for her roles in films such as *The Miracle Worker, The Graduate,* and *84 Charing Cross Road,* and Brenda Vaccaro (*Once Is Not Enough*). As women's roles in society underwent a transformation, Italian-American actresses were also able to change their destiny in the world of cinema. Throughout the thirties, forties, and fifties, the archetype of the femme fatale—beautiful, untouchable, and blessed with everything a man could desire—reigned supreme, but in the second half of the century films began to depict strong, capable, intelligent, pragmatic, and realistic women.

Susan Sarandon, whose mother is Italian American, has emerged as one of the living personifications of the anti-diva. She accepts difficult roles such as the one she played in *Thelma and Louise* (1991), and a nun who acts as the spiritual guide of a death-row inmate in *Dead Man Walking,* for which she won an Academy Award in 1995. Other celebrated actresses are Anjelica Huston (daughter of the acclaimed director John Huston), Beverly D'Angelo, Marisa Tomei, Annabella Sciorra, and more recently Madonna, Mira Sorvino, and Christina Ricci. Also worthy of special mention is Liza Minnelli, a talented singer whose skill as an actress earned her an Academy Award in 1972 for her role as Sally Bowles in the musical film *Cabaret* when she was only in her twenties.

The second half of the twentieth century has undoubtedly been the most prolific time for Italian Americans in cinema. The heritage of great Italian direc-

Left, above: Actor and Academy Award winner Ernest Borgnine, who received an Oscar in 1955 as best actor for his role in *Marty.*

Right, above: Ben Gazzara, a film star of the 1950s and 1960s.

Left, below: Actress Anjelica Huston starred in *Prizzi's Honor,* for which she won the 1995 Academy Award for best supporting actress. Her Italian grandfather Tony Soma, taught her to "stand on her head and sing opera," she says.

Stanley Tucci starred in *Big Night,* a film about two Italian immigrant brothers searching for the American Dream. Tucci, an Emmy Award winning actor, also writes, directs, and produces movies.

tors such as Vincente Minnelli (*An American in Paris*) and Gregory La Cava has been proudly carried on by third-generation directors such as Francis Ford Coppola, Michael Cimino, Brian De Palma, Martin Scorsese, and in the 1990s Quentin Tarantino, Stanley Tucci, Penny Marshall, and Nancy Savoca.

Although some of these directors have caused controversy in the Italian-American community and have been held responsible for the spread of damaging stereotypes regarding their ethnic group, especially the mafioso image, their artistic success is undeniable.

Films such as *The Godfather, Casino,* and *Goodfellas,* the latter based on the reporting and screenwriting on Nicholas Pileggi, were sociologically limited in the sense that they amplified the Mafia phenomenon, which has always represented only a tiny and unworthy minority in a large, hardworking ethnic community. These films also launched the careers of Robert De Niro and Al Pacino, famous for having often played characters linked to the world of gangsters and organized crime, but they also brought new energy to film, introducing a new and difficult type of acting that requires a total immersion of the actor into his role. The same might be said about James Gandolfini, who convincingly runs a

Actor Al Pacino, star of *The Godfather* **and** *Scent of a Woman.*

mob while privately undergoing therapy in the damaging HBO series, "The Sopranos".

The self-made man is another character that appears often in Italian-American cinema, a reflection of the story of many individuals of Italian origins who began with nothing and proved themselves capable of great success. Films such as *Rocky* and its sequels, starring Sylvester Stallone, depicted the common man's rise to glory. The autobiographical element in these films evidently recalls the life of Stallone, who, from a humble and underprivileged background, rose quickly to international fame after his script for *Rocky* was noticed by a powerful film producer.

Left, above: The amusing Danny De Vito, featured in the movies *Tin Men, Twins,* and *Romancing the Stone,* and in the television show "Taxi."

Right, above: Actor Chazz Palminteri.

Left, below: The extraordinary entertainer Jimmy Durante was a vaudeville legend and early television star. Called "Shnozzola" for his enormous nose, he became famous for humorous songs such as "Inka Dinka Doo."

Along with Stallone's strong, muscular characters, Italian-American cinema has also seen the success of comic actors Danny De Vito and Joe Pesci, and actors who slip from comic to dramatic roles with ease, such as Nicolas Cage, Danny Aiello, and Joe Mantegna. The long list of actors continues with Ray Liotta, Ralph Macchio, John Turturro, Chazz Palminteri, and Vincent D'Onofrio, finally arriving at the young movie superstar Leonardo DiCaprio, who starred in *Titanic,* the biggest box-office success in the history of cinema.

John Travolta began his career in the early 1970s performing in television sitcoms and movie musicals. After a temporary loss of momentum in the 1980s, Travolta returned to the spotlight in the film *Pulp Fiction* (1994), directed by Quentin Tarantino. Since then he has acted in other highly successful movies such as *Face-Off,* in which he played opposite Nicolas Cage.

Italian Americans not only have brought their talents to the big screen as actors and directors but also have reached important positions in movie production, in international rights protection organizations, and in the promotion and supervision of the film industry.

Albert R. "Cubby" Broccoli, for example, went down in history as the man who produced the James Bond movies, a series so successful that it is estimated that half the world's population has seen at least one of these films. Before his death in 1996, Broccoli produced all but one of the first seventeen movies about Agent 007, launching in the starring role such famous actors as Sean Connery, Roger Moore, Timothy Dalton, and Pierce Brosnan.

Jack Valenti, president of the Motion Picture Association of America, leads the organization that promotes American films in the United States and internationally and supervises the enormous home-video market as well. Valenti divides his time between an extraordinary political career and the glittering world of cinema. He was friend and advisor to President Lyndon Johnson following President

ARTS AND ENTERTAINMENT

Connie Francis, a popular singer of the 1950s and 1960s, included Italian songs as part of her repertoire.

Sylvester Stallone, who made his fame in *Rocky.* Stallone also wrote the script for *Rocky,* which won an Academy Award for best picture in 1976.

Kennedy's assassination in Dallas, and is still one of the most powerful lobbyists in Washington and most influential players in Hollywood.

Blockbuster, the largest supplier of home videos in the United States, is also headed by an Italian American, John F. Antioco, who serves as chairman and chief executive officer of the company.

THE SOUND OF ITALIAN AMERICANS

Music, along with cinema, is the art form to which Italian Americans have made important contributions. Pop and jazz, like opera, have been deeply influenced by gifted Italian Americans over the course of the twentieth century.

During the wave of immigration that took place around 1880, most Italians settled in the industrial cities along the East Coast, but a smaller number, mostly Sicilians, landed in New Orleans where, at the beginning of the twentieth century, they formed a community of at least 800,000 people. Among them there were musicians drawn by the possibility of performing at the New Orleans French Opera House, which at that time was looking for Italian musicians who alone knew operatic music.

It was in 1913 that this Louisiana city saw the birth of the Original Dixieland Jazz Band, the first music group in the world to call itself a jazz band. The group was formed by Dominick "Nick" LaRocca, a cornet player who was to go down in the history of American music as a pioneer of jazz.

The Original Dixieland Jazz Band was also the first to record a jazz piece ("Darktown Strutters' Ball" in 1917), which sold more than a million records. Although many music critics do not include LaRocca's name in the ranks of the talented originators of jazz, his influence was recognized by the great Louis Armstrong, who remarked that he was fascinated by LaRocca's group even before he began to play the trumpet himself. In a biography, Armstrong stated that "[LaRocca's] fame as one of the great pioneers of syncopated music should last as long as American music lasts."

Jack Valenti, president of the Motion Picture Association of America, with actress Gina Lollobrigida.

The first half of the twentieth century also saw the rise of other important Italian-American jazz musicians. The most representative are Leon Roppolo, a clarinetist, and Joseph "Wingy" Mannone, who lost an arm at the age of twelve and, no longer able to work, began playing the kazoo to support his family. Others include Tony Parenti, a saxophonist and clarinetist; Joe Venuti, the man who introduced the violin in jazz; and Louis Prima, who achieved international popularity with such immortal jazz numbers as "Sing, Sing, Sing" (later recorded by Benny Goodman) and "Angelina."

After World War II, as jazz continued to evolve, adding new expressive outlets, other Italian-American musicians began to emerge. Among the more recent modern jazz musicians are guitarist Bucky Pizzarelli, who passed on his passion for music to his son, John Pizzarelli; singer Morgana King, born Mary Grace Messina, who also appeared in *The Godfather* as Michael Corleone's mother; and trumpet player Chuck Mangione, who became famous with his smooth-jazz hit "Feels So Good."

Jazz has produced numerous talents of Italian descent, but pop music has produced even more, and Italian-American artists in this genre have gained international fame. From the time the first immigrants came to the New World, Americans have always enjoyed "the Italian sound." Italians brought with them a musical heritage consisting of enchanting melodies, heartbreaking romanticism, and a magic borrowed from the operas of Verdi, Puccini, and Donizetti, among others.

One of the first Italian-American pop artists to achieve national success was Russ Colombo, born Ruggiero di Rodolfo Columbo, a young singer with a soft voice who rivaled Bing Crosby in the late 1920s. His accidental death at the age of twenty-six cut short a promising career.

Colombo's style opened the door for other singers of the thirties and forties, including Perry Como (born Pierino Ronald Como) and Frank Sinatra (Francis Albert Sinatra). Although Como sang in a band as early as the 1920s, he did not achieve success until the mid-1940s when, under contract with RCA, he put out his first hit, "Till the End of Time," followed by an unforgettable album entitled *That's My Desire.*

Frank Sinatra remains one of the few singers in the history of American popular music to have enchanted three generations of fans. His unique style and the swing rhythms of his performances have rendered him an icon in the entertainment world. His life, full of artistic successes, both in music and acting, and his determination and self-assurance were all captured in his famous 1968 hit "My Way." Thirty years later he performed in Rio de Janeiro in front of an audience of 170,000 people, creating a world record for the number of people at a concert. When he died in 1998, Sinatra was widely euogized by critics as the greatest popular singer in U.S. history.

Frank Sinatra's generation also produced singer and actor Dean Martin (born Dino Paul Crocetti), who began his career in a partnership with comedian Jerry Lewis and went on to achieve enormous success in music with songs such as "That's Amore," "Volare," and "Everybody Loves Somebody." Other artists, such as Jerry Vale (Gennaro Luigi Vitaliano), Jimmy Roselli (Michael Roselli), and Connie Francis (Concetta Franconero) sang English but also kept alive the music of their roots, sometimes recording songs in Italian— and especially in Sicilian and Neapolitan. Vic Damone (Vito Rocco Farinola) also drew inspiration from Italian music (specifically from Ruggiero Leoncavallo's popular song "Mattinata") for his hit, "You're Breaking My Heart." A generation later, Sergio Franchi continued to popularize Italian romantic music here and abroad.

Singer Tony Bennett (Anthony Dominick Benedetto), winner of numerous Grammy and Emmy awards, has carved a career that has lasted fifty years with no sign of slowing down. Bennett's uninterrupted chain of successes stems from the fact that he has always remained faithful to his own elegant, romantic style, although he has reached out to younger generations by offering modern interpretations of such classics as "Fly Me to the Moon."

After World War II, musical tastes in America slowly changed direction. The crooning style of singers like Sinatra and Como gave way to faster rhythms, and the public lost its taste for big bands. Young Italian-American singers like Frankie Valli, Tommy Sands, Dion and the Belmonts,

Below: Frank Sinatra, singer, film star, and American icon. Nicknamed "Ol' Blue Eyes," "The Voice," and "The Chairman of the Board," he was a giant in American popular culture. After making more than two thousand recordings during a sixty-year career, he died in 1998 at age 82.

Above: Singer Tony Bennett's original name was Anthony Dominick Benedetto.

Left: Perry Como is a singer who has performed worldwide and earned a following of devoted fans, drawn to his warm personality and easy-going ways.

Left: Sonny Bono, who with his wife Cher produced the hit "I Got You, Babe." Later they divorced and Bono entered politics, first becoming mayor of Palm Springs, California, and then a U.S. congressman from California. He died in a skiing accident in 1998.

Right: Dean Martin, the famous singer and film star, was born Dino Paul Crocetti in Ohio.

Frankie Avalon and others became popular. Among them was a singer named Johnny Rae, born John Anthony Pompeo. The increasing popularity of television also contributed to this change, absorbing the attention of the public to such an extent that successful singers were obliged to make frequent television appearances in order to gain visibility. Among those whose fame was guaranteed by television was Sonny Bono (Salvatore Phillip Bono), the author of hits such as "I Got You, Babe" (1965), which he performed with Cher, at the time his partner in music and in marriage.

With the arrival of the 1980s, the world of music was taken by storm by singers such as Madonna (Madonna Veronica Louise Ciccone) and Jon Bon Jovi (John Bongiovani), who became the idols of teenagers all over the world and influenced styles in music and fashion. Bruce Springsteen (whose mother was Italian) took another direction, following in the footsteps of the singer-songwriters of the 1970s, selling millions of copies of his album *Born in the USA* (1984).

ITALIAN AMERICANS IN THE FINE ARTS

Italy has produced some of 65 percent of the world's art. From Giotto to Leonardo da Vinci to Michelangelo to Raphael, Italian artistic talent is recognized the world over. Italian American artists, however, and their contributions, although significant, have been greatly underestimated.

One of the first Italian artists to work in America was Giuseppe Ceracchi, a prolific sculptor who made more than twenty busts of eighteenth-century American politicians, including presidents George Washington and Thomas Jefferson. Ceracchi's bust of the first secretary of the treasury, Alexander Hamilton, served as a source of inspiration for the portrait of him that today appears on the ten-dollar bill.

Another early artistic expression of Italians in America was the Capitol in Washington, for which many Italian artists were recruited at the beginning of the nineteenth century, to give the building a neoclassical look.

The Capitol's architect, Benjamin Latrobe, summoned Giovanni Andrei and Giuseppe Franzoni to the United States for the execution of such sculptural works as the Corinthian columns and the friezes above them. After one of their frequent trips to Italy, Andrei and Franzoni brought back more artists, including Carlo Franzoni, Giuseppe's brother, and a cousin, Francesco Iardella, who executed statues and other decorative works for the famous building.

The construction of the Capitol was a colossal project that took many years, involving other Italian artists, including Enrico Causici and Luigi Persico, who sculpted in sandstone reliefs that depicted significant moments in American history and were located in the rotunda and in the statuary hall. Many of their works deteriorated, however, and some of these were later reproduced in Vermont marble by artists such as George Giannetti.

The Capitol even had its own "Michelangelo," as many called the Italian-American painter Constantino Brumidi. Recognized as the man responsible for decorating the Capitol rotunda's interior dome, Brumidi also frescoed various rooms of the building, including the magnificent President's Room where Lincoln signed the Emancipation Proclamation. He began working on the Capitol dome in 1855 and dedicated the rest of his life to the project. He died in 1880 at age seventy-five.

New York as well was in a frenzy of construction at the end of the nine-

Above: Award-winning conductor and composer Bill Conti has written music for more than seventy films and forty TV shows. His most famous compositions include "Gonna Fly Now" from the film *Rocky* and the score to the James Bond film *For Your Eyes Only*.

Right: Composer and conductor Henry Mancini is best remembered for the song "Moon River" from the film *Breakfast at Tiffany's*. He also wrote the scores for eighty other popular movies.

teenth century, and in that city there were six brothers who made important contributions: Attilio, Ferruccio, Furio, Horatio, Maso, and Orazio Piccirilli, sons of an Italian sculptor who had immigrated to the United States. Having become skilled sculptors in their own right, the Piccirilli brothers opened a studio in New York that became one of the largest and most renowned in the United States. Among the many commissions executed by the Piccirillis under the supervision of the eldest brother, Attilio, were the Lincoln Memorial in Washington, the lions guarding the entrance to the New York Public Library, and some of the statues decorating Rockefeller Center.

The great symbol of America, the Statue of Liberty, also had an Italian among its creators: John Rapetti, whose name is engraved in the crown of the famous statue along with those of his colleagues. In the twentieth century Joseph Nicolosi sculpted portraits of many famous people, including President Franklin Delano Roosevelt, Babe Ruth, and Queen Elizabeth II, in his long and distinguished career.

Italian Americans have been very active in sculpture, but great talents have blossomed in the world of painting as well. Among the most important are Joseph Stella, remembered for his futuristic representations of New York's skyscrapers and bridges; Robert De Niro, father of the famous actor of the same name and author of paintings of great physicality; and Ralph Fasanella, known for a primitivist painting style that featured themes from working-class life and ethnic neighborhoods. More recently, Frank Stella made an important contribution to the Post-Expressionist and abstract movements in American art.

One of the most promising young artists is perhaps Tom DiSalvo, a self-taught Sicilian-American painter whose art is a synthesis and free interpretation of futurism, pop art, and academic representational art.

ARTS AND
ENTERTAINMENT
123

THE ETERNAL

POETS AND WRITERS

It is not surprising that during the nineteenth century and at the beginning of the twentieth century there were few noteworthy examples of Italian-American poets and writers. A study conducted at the end of the 1940s found only fifty-nine. A primary reason for this apparent dearth of writers is the fact that, as we have already seen, the immigrants who came to the United States had little education, and their need to work distanced them from the possibility of extensive schooling.

Not all Italians who arrived in the United States were totally uneducated, however. Some had the good fortune to have studied in Italy; others reached an adequate level of education in their new land. In some cases, would-be writers and intellectuals could be found even among miners, railroad laborers, and traveling salesmen. But usually their need to work for a living was so imperative they had no other choice but to renounce their artistic aspirations. Few had the luck to hold on to their dreams and succeed.

It was a work environment of degradation and at times inhumane misery that gave rise to one of the most important writers of the early twentieth century, Pascal D'Angelo. His story, similar to many others, began in 1910, when he immigrated to the United States with his father at the age of sixteen. When his father decided to return to Italy, D'Angelo remained in America, certain that somewhere there was a place for him to cultivate his lifelong passion for literature. After many years of labor and numerous rejections from newspaper and magazine editors, he found his Pygmalion in the editor Carl Van Doren, who was the first to believe in the writer's talent and who published *Son of Italy*, D'Angelo's autobiography, which was successful.

Other talented authors shared experiences like D'Angelo's, searching for and finding fortune through literature in the United States. Two of these are Constantine Panunzio, who described an American adventure steeped in dreams, frustration, and powerful sentiments in his autobiography, *Soul of an Immigrant,* and Emanuele Carnevali, whose collection of short stories entitled *A Hurried Man* is a touching depiction of the strong feelings of ambivalence that immigrants often experience.

The classic novel *Christ in Concrete,* by Pietro Di Donato, tells a difficult story of immigration through the tragic account of a father's accidental death in the workplace. Other noteworthy literary figures include John Fante (*Wait Until*

Italian-American sculptor Joseph Nicolosi with his *Life Eternal.* Nicolosi was born in Italy in 1893 and came to the United States in 1912. He is well known for his major commissions in the United States and Europe.

Left: Gay Talese is the best-selling author of many highly praised titles, including *Honor Thy Father, Unto the Sons,* and *The Kingdom and the Power.*

Right: Jerre Mangione (1909-1998) was one of the most celebrated early Italian-American writers. He co-authored, with Ben Morreale, the critically acclaimed *La Storia: Five Centuries of the Italian American Experience*, a monumental five-century social history of the Italians in America.

Spring, Bandini), the poet and critic John Ciardi, Jerre Mangione (author of *Mount Allegro* and *La Storia,* written with Ben Morreale), and Guido D'Agostino (*Olives on the Apple Tree*).

In recent times, Italian-American women in literature have won critical attention. Helen Barolini, for example, is a prolific writer, critic, and poet whose novel *Umbertina* explores the ties among four generations of Italian-American women. Other important modern Italian American writers are novelist Barbara Grizzuti Harrison, poet Diane Di Prima, and authors Camille Paglia, Anne Paolucci, and Rina Ferrarelli, who have chosen to write about themes not exclusively centered on the Italian-American experience.

Among contemporary writers, one of the most important and well-established is Gay Talese, a journalist, historian, and acute observer of the evolving reality of Americans and Italian Americans. Having grown up with a pervasive sensation of being an outsider, Talese used his writing talent to vindicate common people who were not allowed to express their opinions, as in his book *Fame and Obscurity.* Although he has written on many topics over the course of his career, Talese has also explored the Italian-American experience. In *Unto the Sons,*

Talese tells the history of his family in the United States and in their native Calabria, revealing an often hard reality of poverty and degradation yet always imbuing it with intense sentiments.

A contemporary of Talese, Don DeLillo, is regarded by many critics as one of the most significant American novelists of the twentieth century. His books—from *Americana, Jones, Street,* and *White Noise* to *Libra* and *Underworld*—have been universally acclaimed, and he has won the National Book Award and the PEN/Faulkner Award for fiction.

In comparison with the past century, today there are many more Italian-American authors who represent their ethnic group and its historic journey. Although not all modern-day Italian American writers choose to deal with themes directly related to their heritage, many continue to tell tales of immigration and sacrifice, of success and great accomplishments. These voices are fundamentally important if we want to remember the past and make the most of the present. The work of these artists confirms that the nation's Italian-American community is not destined to disappear into the landscape of twenty-first-century America.

John Ciardi, an accomplished poet, scholar, and writer, was born in 1916 to an immigrant Italian family and went on to teach at Harvard. Ciardi, who died in 1986, also won recognition for his English translation of Dante's *Divine Comedy*, the only English translation to use Dante's complex rhyme scheme.

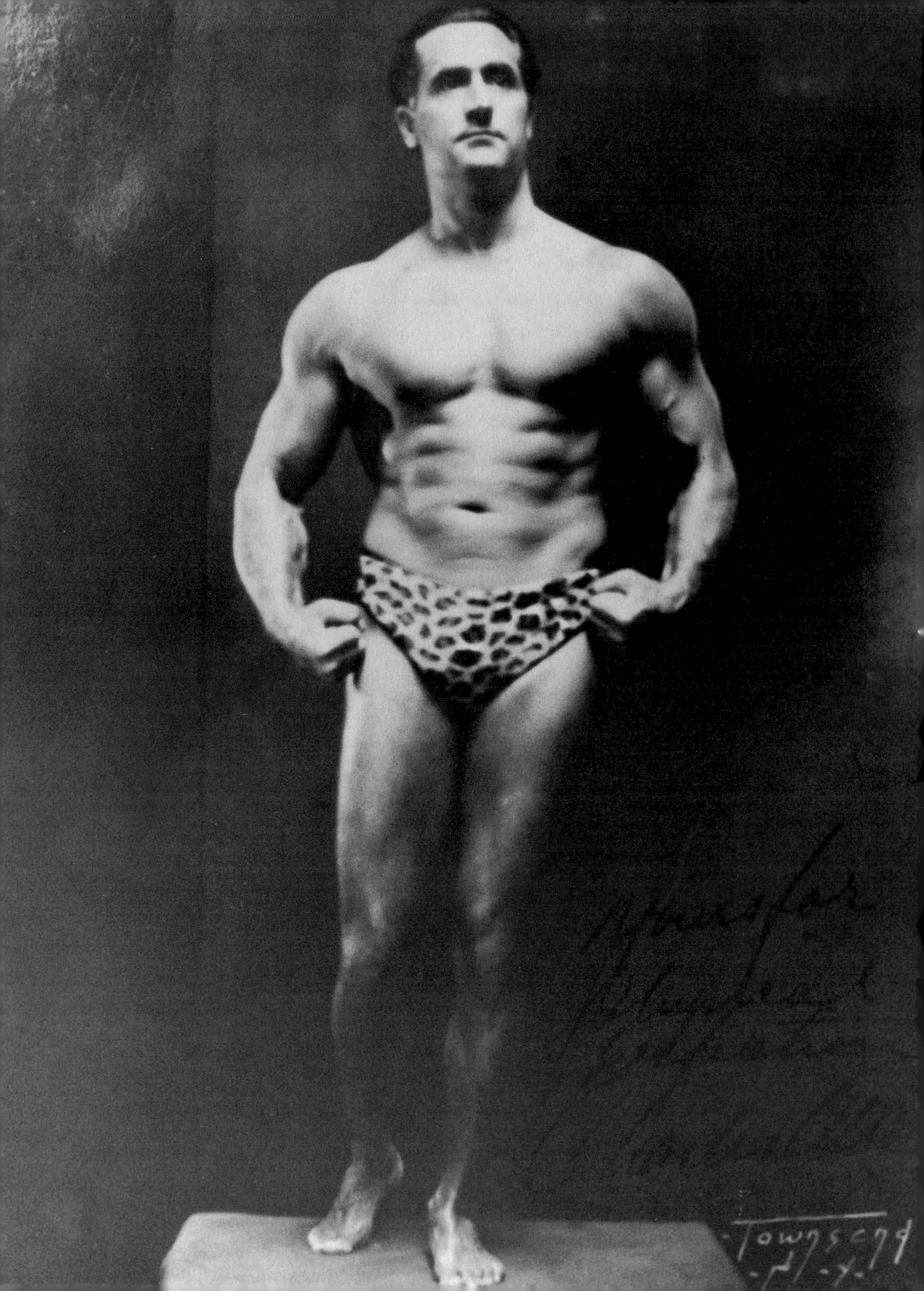
Townsend
N.Y.

SPORTS

A LEVEL PLAYING FIELD

Many early Italian immigrants to the United States first became familiar with America through faded daguerreotypes that circulated in their little towns, showing vast Western landscapes and illustrations of the Statue of Liberty torn from flyers that guaranteed plenty of work, opportunity, and happiness in the New World. What they found upon arriving did not exactly conform to these images.

Here in "the New World," they were herded into urban ghettoes and singled out for insults because of their dark features and foreign speech. Witnesses to a widespread xenophobia that was often open and sometimes covert, the children of these new arrivals were determined to fit in one way or another. At school they learned about the American Revolution rather than the Italian Renaissance. At home they answered their parents in English. The girls wanted to be like Mary Pickford, Lillian Gish, and other American actresses, while the boys soon realized that sports could help make them more American.

And so they played baseball, football, and basketball—the sports that the Americans were crazy about, whose players, they discovered, were admired above all other men. Italian Americans, too, fell in love with these sports and athletes. Eventually this fascination with American sports produced many great Italian-American athletes who, in turn, helped Italian Americans gain the respect of the larger American society.

A man from California changed everything in the 1940s. Concluding a thir-

Muscle man Charles Atlas, born Angelo Siciliano, invented the bodybuilding technique called isometrics in 1921. By the 1950s he had cultivated a great following.

teen-season baseball career with a .325 lifetime batting average, Joseph Paul DiMaggio was perhaps America's most admired and loved athlete. Yet DiMaggio was also an Italian American, a son of a poor Sicilian immigrant. With DiMaggio, Italian Americans had their first cultural hero. He was followed by many other Italian Americans in many other sports, as we shall see in this chapter.

BASEBALL GREATS

Italian Americans have supplied talent for the great American pastime nearly since its beginnings in 1846. "Buttercup" Dickerson, born Lewis Passano, was the first Italian American to play for the majors. He began his career in 1878 as the starting outfielder for Cincinnati. He was only nineteen at the time. A year later he led the National League in triples, scoring a total of 14. On June 16, 1881, he became only the fifth player on record to go 6 for 6 at the plate. Over his seven-year career with the majors, Dickerson obtained a lifetime batting average of .284, an impressive figure even by today's standards.

Little if anything is known about Dickerson's Italian heritage, and he no doubt preferred to keep it that way. An Italian surname during this period meant limits; it meant having to confine oneself to the harsh and unfair stereotypes projected by the majority American class. It would be several decades before an Italian American could speak his name aloud with pride.

The 1920s produced some of baseball's finest athletes, as well as some of the best teams to grace the diamond. But in a decade of greats, the New York Yankees consistently outshone every team they played. Fronting high-profile sluggers such as Babe Ruth and Lou Gehrig, the 1920s Yankees seemed almost unstoppable, and during the famed 1927 season they indeed *were* unstoppable. While Ruth and Gehrig may have captured the public limelight of that year's "murderer's row," another man, the youngest on the team, quietly helped drive the Yankees to a World Series championship.

Tony "Poosh 'Em Up" Lazzeri, whose career spanned from 1926 through 1939, was the Yankees' second baseman and one of the smartest players in baseball. The Yankees acquired Lazzeri from Salt Lake City, a team in the minor Pacific Coast League, after he set records that year by hitting 60 HR, 222 RBI, and 202 runs, the later of which still stands. Lazzeri acquired his nickname, "Poosh 'Em Up" Tony, while playing for Salt Lake when an Italian-American restaurant

Joe DiMaggio with his wife Marilyn Monroe. Known as "The Yankee Clipper," he was the son of Sicilian immigrants. DiMaggio was voted "Greatest Living Player" of baseball in 1955 and inducted into the Baseball Hall of Fame only four years after he retired. He died in 1999.

SPORTS
131

owner gave him free spaghetti dinners during a hitting slump to help him "Poosh 'Em Up," or to hit. Despite his stunning success in the Pacific League, many teams shied away from purchasing Lazzeri because of his epileptic condition. Lazzeri never had a seizure while on the field, and is one of fewer than twenty players to have played every game his rookie year.

Lazzeri made very few errors per season and was widely considered the best second baseman in the league, as well as the Yankees' best infielder. He was just as good behind the plate, batting .300 or better in six seasons and obtaining more than 100 RBI in seven.

Lazzeri was a quiet man who let his athletic intelligence and skill rather than his mouth do the talking. Amidst his more boisterous teammates, he was never a favorite of the press, who claimed that interviewing him was "like trying to mine coal with a nail file." But despite his rather taciturn approach to the game, he is still notable for his leadership both on and off the field. Umpire Tommy Connolly once observed, "When things get tough out there, the others don't look to Ruth or any of the veterans. They look to [Lazzeri], and he never fails them."

And fail them he did not, excelling even late in his career. On May 24, 1936, he became the first player to hit two grand slams in one game, and he subsequently set an American League record of 11 RBI. He ended his career with a .292 batting average, 178 home runs, more than 1,000 RBI, and having appeared in seven World Series. In 1991 he was posthumously inducted into the Baseball Hall of Fame by the Committee on Baseball Veterans.

Lazzeri was not only a role model for ballplayers, but a role model for the Italian-American community as well. He hailed from San Francisco and worked with his father as a boilermaker on the off seasons, even after ascending to the majors. The New York Italian Americans absolutely loved Lazzeri, as he was the first truly conspicuous Italian-American sports hero, and even held a Tony Lazzeri Day in his honor at Yankee Stadium on September 8, 1927.

While Lazzeri captured the hearts of New York fans during the twenties and thirties, it would still be a decade before an Italian-American athlete would gain the respect of the nation—and the world. Even as Lazzeri and the Yankees belted out home run after home run, the young DiMaggio brothers were perfecting their swings in the sandlots of California. Their father, a Sicilian immigrant who ran a fishing boat off the coast of San Francisco, did not approve of his sons' passion for baseball, calling it "a bum's game," and urged them to instead follow him into the fishing business.

Luckily for themselves and for America, they did not listen. Vincent DiMaggio, the eldest of the three DiMaggio boys, was a two-time all-star who played ten seasons in the National League for Boston, Cincinnati, Pittsburgh, and New York. Vince had his best season in 1941, hitting 21 home runs and 100 RBI.

Seven-time all-star Dominic, the youngest DiMaggio, played in the outfield next to the legendary Ted Williams. Dom had a lifetime batting average of .298, and averaged 103 runs per season while he played for the Boston Red Sox in the 1940s. Known as "The Little Professor" because of the spectacles he wore, Dom nevertheless proved himself quite the athlete. He hit in thirty-four straight games in 1949 and in twenty-seven straight in 1951, and still holds the American League record for putouts by an outfielder, racking up 503 in one season.

The middle brother, Joseph DiMaggio, was a particularly shy man, not given much to bragging as some of his teammates were, or even to conversing with people outside his close circle of friends. And yet Americans absolutely loved him, and they continued to proclaim him the greatest living ballplayer for nearly half a century after his retirement.

How could the son of a poor Italian immigrant rise to the upper echelons of American pop culture? One obvious answer was Joe DiMaggio's unparalleled grace both on and off the field, a grace that the media and the fans were quick to notice and admire. From his wide, smooth swing to his effortless catches in center field, DiMaggio made everything look easy. While a great deal of this was due to natural ability, it was also because DiMaggio had a flawless work ethic, devoting countless hours to studying plays and perfecting his throwing arm. His legendary fifty-six-game hitting streak in the summer of 1941 seemed almost effortless, and indeed it may have been, as immediately after the streak he again hit consecutive runs, this time for sixteen straight games. No player has gotten within ten games of his record.

In 1934 the New York Yankees signed DiMaggio away from his minor league team, the San Francisco Seals, after he batted safely in sixty-one consecutive games. Other teams had been avoiding DiMaggio because he had recently injured his leg, but the Yankees snatched him up, paying only $25,000 for him, a

SPORTS
134

very low price for a player of such obvious talent. It was one of the best deals they ever made. In his rookie year, 1936, DiMaggio batted .323, hit 29 HR, 125 RBI, and set AL rookie records with runs (132) and triples (15). The fans instantly loved him. DiMaggio played for the Yankees his entire career, from 1936 through 1951, only taking off three years of his prime to serve in World War II. Had he not served his country, he would have no doubt broken more records.

Off the field, DiMaggio was equally endearing to the public. They liked his soft-spoken manner and unwillingness to promote his own athletic reputation. His 1954 celebrity marriage to Marilyn Monroe, the great American sex symbol, increased his fame dramatically. The marriage ended in divorce less than a year later but still survives in American history as one of the highlights of popular culture.

If DiMaggio's pop-star status proclaims his greatness, his baseball statistics certainly prove it. "Joltin' Joe" had a lifetime batting average of .325, with 1,537 runs batted in and 361 home runs, an amazing figure for a right-handed hitter who played half of his games in Yankee Stadium, which was notoriously unfriendly to right-handed batters. In 1938 he finished the season with an incredible .381 batting average. The Yankee Clipper was named the Associated Press Athlete of the Year in 1941 and voted the American League Most Valuable Player in 1939, 1941, and 1947. He led the Yankees to ten pennant and nine World Series championships, becoming the first player to appear in more than fifty World Series games. DiMaggio retired in 1951 after his fifty-first World Series game appearance and was inducted into the Baseball Hall of Fame in 1955. In 1978 he became the first inductee into the National Italian American Sports Hall of Fame in Chicago.

Whereas DiMaggio charmed the nation with his grace, Lawrence Peter Berra delighted it with his wit. Only five-foot-eight and built like a stump, this St. Louis native seemed an unlikely hero for a team that had once fielded greats such as DiMaggio and Ruth. Nevertheless, Berra proved himself more than able to fill the colossal shoes of his predecessors, leading the Yankees, with whom he would spend his entire career, to a record ten World Series championships during his career (1946–63.) He played in a total of seventy-five World Series games, with 259 at-bats, 71 hits, and 10 doubles—all World Series records.

Berra, who was nicknamed Yogi because he sat in the dugout with his legs

Ballplayer Billy Martin (born Alfred Manuel Pesano) was also a manager of the New York Yankees. He was the first Italian-American manager to win a World Series, leading the Yankees to victory in 1977.

Left: Joe Torre as a young baseball player. He is now manager of the New York Yankees.

Below: Yogi Berra, playing for the New York Yankees, is safe at third base, 1949. One of baseball's greatest catchers, he later managed the Yankees and the Mets. In 1964, when he led the Yankees to win the pennant, he became the first Italian-American manager to win a league championship.

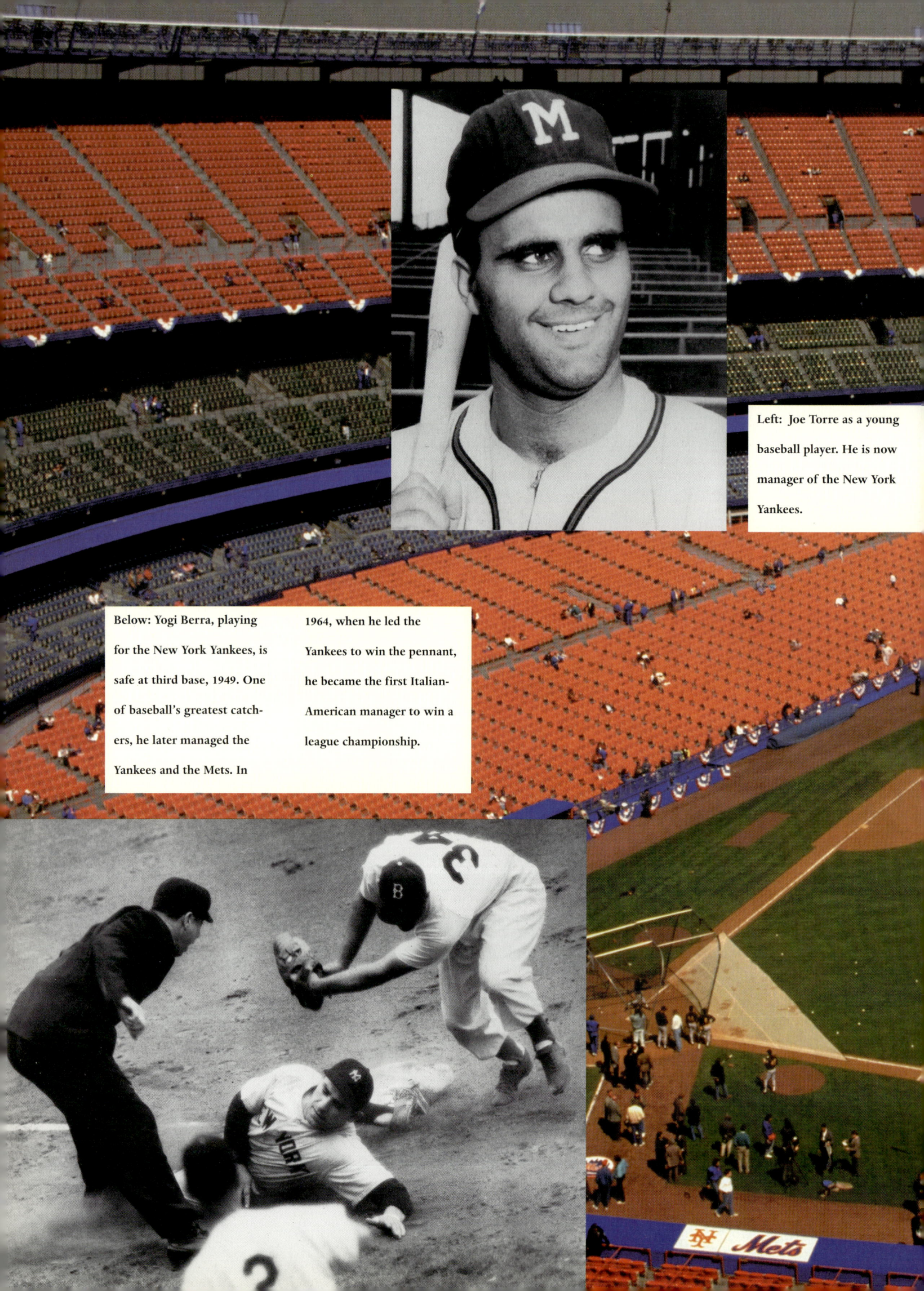

Above: Baseball player Mike Piazza is catcher for the New York Mets.

crossed like an Indian snake charmer, began his career with the Yankees as an outfielder but quickly moved behind the plate as catcher. Berra had been a good outfielder, but he was a phenomenal catcher. He could jump on a bunt quicker than anyone in the league and, with an extremely powerful and accurate arm to back him up, he could throw out even the fastest runner. He had an impeccable sense of pitch calling, and in 1958 he became one of only five catchers ever to achieve a perfect fielding percentage of 1.000. As a batter, Berra could hit almost any pitch, including the bad ones. In 1950 he struck out only twelve times at 597 at-bats. He was also voted an American League Most Valuable Player on three occasions. Berra went on to coach for the Yankees, the Mets, and the Astros, becoming one of only a handful of managers to win pennants in both leagues, and was inducted into the Baseball Hall of Fame in 1972.

Berra is remembered best for his comical turns of phrase. When told by a teammate that a game they were playing was as good as finished, he told him, "It ain't over till it's over," a phrase that has since become part of America's pop philosophy. He also once said, "Baseball is 90 percent mental; the other half is physical."

The son of a New York City trolley conductor, Phil "Scooter" Rizzuto followed in DiMaggio's footsteps as an Italian American who rose from a poor background to achieve nationwide admiration. The Yankees drafted the shortstop in 1941, just as their old shortstop, Frankie Crosetti, had begun to decline with age. This was an excellent break for Rizzuto, who was moved into the starting position. From there, Rizzuto launched a brilliant career. Rizzuto's best year, 1950, saw him awarded the American League MVP award for batting a career high .324 and for his brilliant play during the Yankees' sweep of Phillies. Rizzuto played for the Yankees until 1956. After retiring as a player, Rizzuto moved up to the Yankees' broadcasting booth, where he became an instant hit with the fans. Any disciple of baseball can identify him by his frequent use of the expression "Holy Cow!"

At a time when Italian Americans were still struggling with prejudice because of their names and African Americans because of their skin color, Roy Campanella entered the baseball diamond with both an Italian name and an African skin color. Campanella, a Philadelphian whose father was Italian and whose mother was black, was an impressive athlete from an early age. In 1937 he began his career at age fifteen as catcher with the Baltimore Elite Giants of the Negro National League, for whom he played part-time during the weekends since he was still in school. Soon Campanella quit school to play baseball full-time. By the time he left the Negro League in 1945, he had racked up an MVP and was widely considered the league's best catcher.

In the late 1940s, the Brooklyn Dodgers made the first push to integrate baseball, signing Roy Campanella, Jackie Robinson, and other talented players of the Negro League to their team. Once in Major League Baseball, Campanella proved himself one of the best catchers in the nation, winning the MVP award in 1951, 1953, and 1955. In his best year, 1953, Campanella scored 103 runs, with 142 RBI and 41 HR, both records for catchers. He achieved a lifetime batting average of .276, with 242 HR and 856 RBI.

Campanella overcame a series of injuries late in his career but, tragically, in January 1958 a car accident left him paralyzed from the neck down. Though unable to play, he continued to serve the Dodgers through public relations. Campanella was inducted into the Baseball Hall of Fame in 1969.

Rocky "The Rock" Colavito, born Rocco Domenico, is perhaps the Cleveland Indians' most popular player ever. A product of the Bronx, the handsome power hitter had already reached the 300 HR mark by the time he was thirty-two (in 1965). He hit 40 HR in two consecutive seasons, 1958 and 1959, and was the first Indian to do so. On June 10, 1959, Colavito made history when he slammed four homers in four consecutive at-bats during Cleveland's game against Baltimore. He also had a strong and accurate throwing arm, easily hurling pitches from deep in the field and, if necessary, playing relief pitcher.

"Don't Knock the Rock," fans would say whenever criticism would arise at one of Colavito's frequent batting slumps. To the fans' horror, in 1960 General

Tommy LaSorda, left, celebrated fifty years with the Dodgers in 1999. He has been a player, scout, coach, manager, and vice president. Often called "Mr. Baseball," he managed in three World Series games and three All-Star games.

SPORTS

140

Baseball Hall of Famer Phil Rizzuto was known as "The Scooter" for his talent as shortstop. He played for the Yankees between 1941 and 1954, and was part of ten pennant-winning seasons and nine World Series classics. After retiring, he became "The Voice of the Yankees" as a sports announcer.

Manager Frank Lane traded Colavito to Detroit in return for power hitter Harvey Kuenn. The trade was a disaster. Cleveland slumped into several decades of bad playing, and Colavito moved on to his best season, hitting 45 home runs and batting .290 with 140 RBI in 1961 for Detroit.

Baseball fans knew "Battlin'" Billy Martin, born Alfred Manuel Pesano, because of his infamous temper. But behind his fiery personality lurked a talented ballplayer and, later in his life, an effective coach. Martin's career spanned more than a decade, beginning in 1950 and ending in 1961, during which he played for the Yankees, the Tigers, and the Indians. As a second baseman for the Yankees, Martin's competitive style made him a favorite of manager Casey Stengel. Unfortunately, in 1957 Stengel was forced to trade Martin to the Tigers after a nightclub brawl involving Martin and several other Yankees. Just a year before, Martin had achieved a career high, hitting 75 RBI and 15 HR.

In 1969 Martin took up managing for the Minnesota Twins and established a careerlong pattern of first guiding his team to victory and then getting himself fired. Martin traveled from team to team for several decades, managing the Yankees on five separate occasions, including a stint in 1977 in which he lunged at Yankees star Reggie Jackson on national television during a World Series game. The Yankees won the championship, but owner George Steinbrenner fired him a year later. The Yankees hired Martin again in 1979, but then fired him once more after he beat up a marshmallow salesman. This pattern continued for some time until 1988, when the Yankees fired him for good after he was involved in the very activity that got him kicked off the team in the first place—a nightclub tussle. Despite all this, Martin was a successful manager, winning Manager of the Year in 1974, 1976, 1980, and 1981, and division crowns in 1969 with Minnesota, 1972 with Detroit, 1976 and 1977 with the Yankees, and in 1981 with Oakland.

Tommy Lasorda was one of the most popular managers of his time, directing the Dodgers for twenty seasons (1976–1996), one of only four managers to manage the same team for so long. Lasorda began as a promising young player from the Canadian-American league who turned out to be a bust when he was signed by the Dodgers in 1954 as a pitcher. Lasorda drifted into to the minors but returned to the Dodgers in 1961, this time as a scout. In the early 1970s he was signed as a coach and was soon promoted to manager. The Dodgers excelled under Lasorda, winning eight National League West titles, four National League pennants, two World Series championships, and a grand total of 1,599 games before his retirement. Lasorda was elected to the National Baseball Hall of Fame in 1997.

It took some time for Brooklyn native Joe Torre to earn distinction as a manager. But when he did it, he did it with style. Torre entered baseball in 1960 as a player—a catcher for the Braves who started off very strongly and was voted runner-up to the 1961 National League Rookie of the Year. He made the All-Stars from 1963 to 1967, and won the Gold Glove in 1965. Torre continued to perform after he was traded to the Cardinals, making the All-Star team from 1970 through 1973 and obtaining the MVP award in 1971. He was traded to the Mets following the 1974 season, where his level of play reduced dramatically. In 1977 the Mets moved him into the dugout for good, as their new manager. Despite the slump in the final years of his playing career, Torre still retired with a .297 lifetime average.

A slow starter as manager, Torre could only push the Mets as far as a fourth-place finish over the next five seasons. He managed the Braves until 1984, leading them to a division title and two second-place finishes, but was ultimately fired after a 80–82 season record. Torre returned to New York in 1996, but at the helm of the Yankees. This time he produced results. The Yankees finished first in their division that season and captured the World Series Championship, a feat they had not performed since 1978.

They repeated history in 1998, finishing the season with a .704 win percentage, one of the most outstanding accomplishments in sports history, and then had another knockout season the following year when they once again won the World Series. Needless to say, Joe Torre remains a very popular man in New York—at least among those who aren't Mets fans.

FOOTBALL

By the time the first Italian-American superstars had donned a major-league uniform, baseball was already a well-established sport with a large fan base. But during the slow ascendancy of football in this country, Italian Americans would have the opportunity to alter the very nature of the sport.

American football evolved from college rugby and soccer in the late 1800s. One of the earliest professional teams, the Latrobe Athletic Club in Pennsylvania,

Dan Marino was quarterback for the Miami Dolphins until his retirement after the 1999–2000 season.

SPORTS
143

Right: Football great Franco Harris, a black Italian American, played for the Pittsburgh Steelers. In 1975 he set the record for most yards gained in a Super Bowl—158 against the Minnesota Vikings.

Center: Joe Montana, long-time quarterback of the San Francisco Forty-niners, won four Super Bowl titles. In the year 2000, Montana was inducted into the Football Hall of Fame.

Far right: The legendary coach of the Green Bay Packers, Vince Lombardi, whose motto was "Winning isn't everything. It's the only thing."

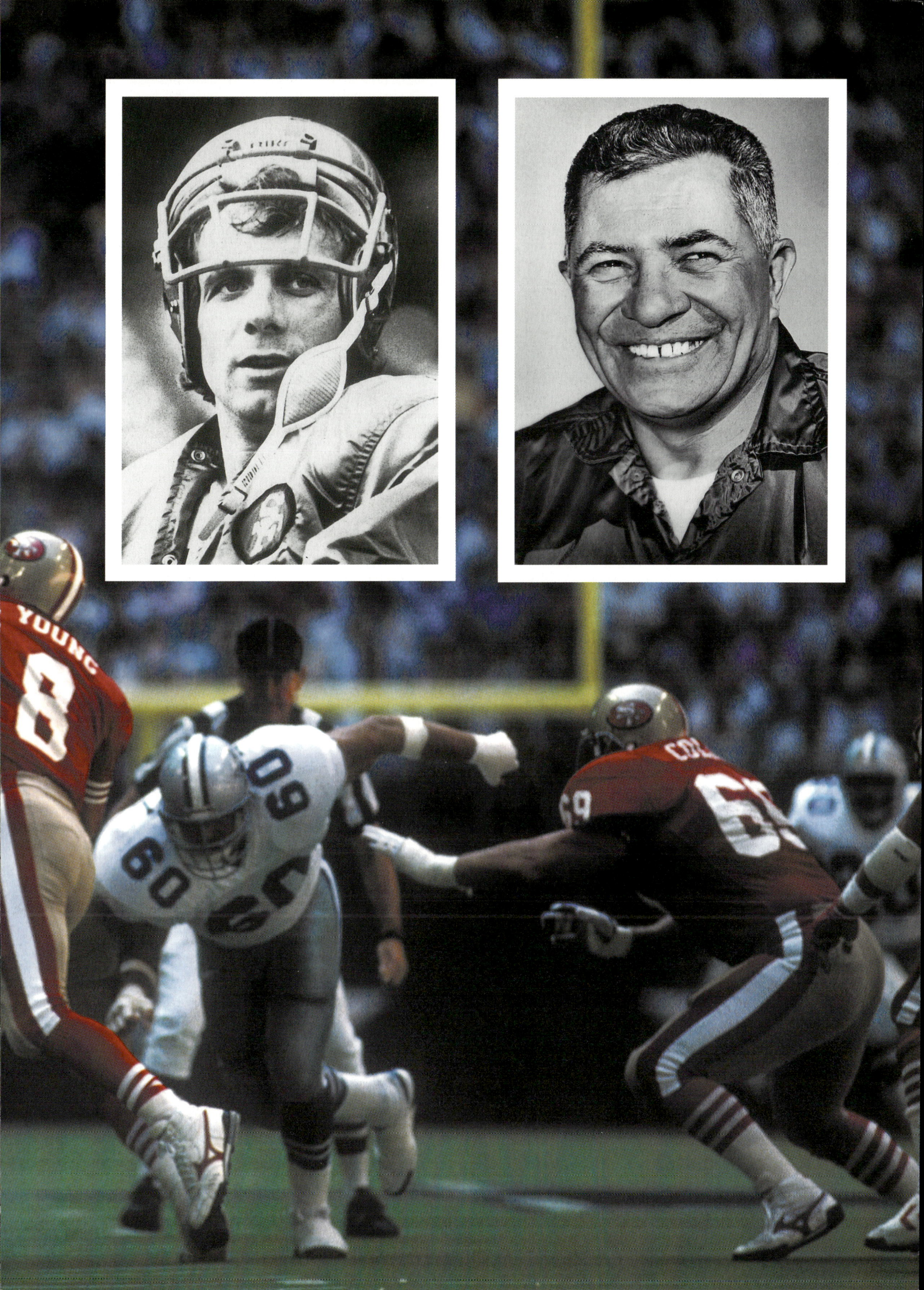
YOUNG
8
60

signed Ed Abbaticchio, the first Italian-American professional football player, as a fullback in 1897. The journalist and former football competitor Fielding Yost credited Abbaticchio with inventing the spiral kick.

In 1897 Abbatichio joined the Phillies as their second baseman. He was the first player to have played both football and baseball, as well as the first somewhat famous baseball player of obvious Italian heritage. He earned a lifetime batting average of .254 over an eight-season career, and eventually signed with the Pittsburgh Pirates, teaming up with legendary shortstop Honus Wagner to form an overpowering double-play combination.

After World War II, during which sports had all but disappeared from the national scene, football's fan base skyrocketed and its new popularity began to encroach on that of baseball.

By virtue of their amazing athletic prowess, several Italian-American football players became some of the sport's first superstars. Charley Trippi, for example, was a key member of the famed Chicago Cardinals' "Dream Backfield" and their number-one future draft pick of 1945. This Georgia All-American helped lead his team to their last NFL title in 1947 when he scored two touchdowns. In a time when versatility among football players was common, Trippi was one of the most versatile of all. He played halfback for five years, quarterback for two years, and defense for two years, for a total of nine seasons, and was enshrined in the Pro Football Hall of Fame in 1968.

Few defensive ends today can even compare to Gino Marchetti, and indeed none could in his day, as he was named the top defensive end of the NFL's first fifty years as well as a Hall of Famer. Marchetti, born in Smithers, West Virginia, was the New York Yanks' number-two draft pick of 1952. The franchise was moved to Dallas in his rookie season, but he did not stay there, moving on to the Baltimore Colts, for whom he excelled. He made the Pro Bowl eleven consecutive times and the All-NFL seven times. Together with quarterback Johnny Unitas, Marchetti drove the Colts to win the 1958 NFL championship and was subsequently named the NFL Player of the Year.

Vince Lombardi is perhaps the greatest and most competitive coach of any sport. A deeply religious man from Brooklyn, he worked Bible quotations into his pregame speeches and espoused a driven and single-minded approach to victory. "Winning is not a sometime thing; it's an all-the-time thing," he once said.

"There is no room for second place." In 1959, only his first year of coaching, Lombardi turned the decimated Green Bay Packers around, improving their record from 1–10 in the previous season to 7–5. From then on, Lombardi and the Packers continued to dominate the NFL, garnering six divisional and five NFL championships in fewer than ten seasons and winning the first two Super Bowls.

Lombardi coached until 1968, then moved into the Green Bay front office as general manager. He could not stay away from coaching for long, though; he accepted a job as coach for the Washington Redskins in 1969, leading them to their first winning season in fourteen years. Unfortunately, Lombardi was soon diagnosed with cancer and had to leave football. He died on September 3, 1970, and was posthumously inducted into the Football Hall of Fame a year later.

Two other Italian-American football players worthy of mention are Andy Robustelli and Franco Harris. "Iron Man" Robustelli, defensive end for the Rams, played in eight NFL title games and seven Pro Bowls. Extremely quick and strong and exceptionally intelligent on the field, he made the All-NFL for seven years and was even named the NFL's top player of 1962 by Maxwell Club. Over his fourteen-year career, Robustelli missed only one game, an amazing accomplishment in such an injury-prone sport. He was inducted into the Football Hall of Fame in 1971.

Penn State star running back Franco Harris signed with the Pittsburgh Steelers in 1972 and quickly proved himself, becoming the NFL Rookie of the Year. Over his career, which lasted through 1984, Harris racked up 12,120 yards rushing, the third-greatest yardage in the history of the NFL, as well as four Super Bowl rings. He was inducted into the Hall of Fame in 1990.

In 1935 the Downtown Athletic Club in New York began awarding the DAC Trophy to collegiate football players who exhibited a high level of achievement in the sport. Seven Italian-American players have won what is now called the Heisman Trophy: Notre Dame's Angelo Bertelli in 1943, Wisconsin's Alan Ameche in 1954, the Naval Academy's Joe Bellino in 1960 (the first from his school to win the award), UCLA's Gary Beban in 1967, John Cappelletti from Paterno's Penn State in 1973, and Miami's Vinnie Testaverde and Gino Torretta in 1986 and 1992 respectively.

Every pro football player has his roots playing for a college team, but few have had the honor of playing for Penn State's Joe Paterno. The 1986 *Sports*

Illustrated Sportsman of the Year has won more than two hundred games in over twenty years, and has led the Nittany Lions to twenty-two postseason bowl games. A three-time Coach of the Year, Paterno won the school's first national championship in the 1982 Sugar Bowl and then went on to upset the University of Miami and its Heisman Trophy winner, Vinnie Testaverde, for the national title only four years later.

Joe Montana is widely considered to be the greatest quarterback of all time. Before joining the NFL, Joseph Clifford Montana, a native of New Eagle, Pennsylvania, played football for Notre Dame. Not always their starter, he still won recognition for his ability to rally the team to victory when off the bench. He brought Notre Dame back to win 35–34 from a 23-point deficit in the fourth quarter of the 1979 Cotton Bowl.

A third-round choice of the San Francisco Forty-niners in the NFL college draft, Montana took over as starter in his second season, leading the league in completions with 64.5 percent for that year. The following season, he led the Forty-niners to the Super Bowl, where they beat the Cincinnati Bengals 26–21, largely due to Montana's 63.6 percent completion rate. For his excellent performance, Montana was named the game's MVP. He led the Forty-niners to three more Super Bowl victories and was named MVP in two of those games. When Montana retired from football in 1994, he had passed for more than 40,000 yards and had played in seven Pro Bowls. He was enshrined into the Hall of Fame on July 29, 2000.

Dan Marino, another great passer, recently retired from football, leaving in his wake some twenty-three NFL passing records, including passing yardage (61,361), career completions (4,967), career touchdown passes (420), passing yards in a season (5,084), and touchdown passes in a season (48). Born in Pittsburgh, Marino played quarterback on his school's team, for which his father also coached. Marino excelled at high school baseball as well as football, and was even given an offer to play professional baseball by the Kansas City Royals. He opted instead to attend the University of Pittsburgh on a football scholarship.

Marino led the Pittsburgh Panthers to a Sugar Bowl Victory, and set school records for career passing yards (8,597), touchdown passes (79), and passes completed (693). After college, Marino was recruited to play professional football by the Miami Dolphins. He quickly replaced aging star quarterback David Woodley and, guided by coach Don Shula, transformed football into a pass-offensive game. From 1984 through 1993, the "Man with the Golden Arm" started in 155 consecutive games for the Miami Dolphins before being plagued with health problems. He announced his retirement in 2000.

BOXING

The 1930s ushered in the first great Italian-American boxer, Tony Canzoneri. Winning the New York State amateur bantamweight championship in 1923, Canzoneri turned professional only a few years later. At age nineteen, he battled Bud Taylor for the world bantamweight championship, but the title proved elusive for the teenager as he fought Taylor to a draw in the first match and then lost to him on a decision in the second. Despite losing these bouts, Canzoneri gained a reputation as a clever fighter as well as a solid hitter.

Rocky Marciano, the only undefeated heavyweight boxing champion in history, retired in 1956 with a record that included forty-three knockouts. He was elected into the Boxing Hall of Fame in 1959. Marciano—born Rocco Marchegiano—was killed in a plane crash.

Canzoneri moved to the featherweight division in 1928, where he won the world title in a sixteen-round decision over Benny Bass. He lost the title that same year to Andre Routis in a ten-round decision. Moving up again in class, Canzoneri captured the lightweight title in 1930 when he knocked out Al Singer, the heavy favorite, in one round. In 1931 he gained yet another title, the junior welterweight championship, by defeating Jack "Kid" Berg with a third-round kayo. Canzoneri lost the title a year later in a ten-round decision to Johnny Jadick, only to win it again from Battling Shaw in 1933. He later lost both the lightweight and junior welterweight titles to Barney Ross, but captured the lightweight title again from Lou Ambers after Ross moved to the welterweights. He again lost the lightweight title, this time to Lou Ambers and was not able to win it back. In 1939, after getting kayoed for the first time, Canzoneri retired from boxing with a career record of 139–24–10 with 44 knockouts and having won titles from three different divisions. Always popular with fans, Canzoneri went on to become a successful actor and restaurateur.

Willie Pep, born Guiglermo Papaleo, is arguably the cleverest and most subtle fighter in boxing history. He was extremely quick on his feet and could easily avoid most punches without retreating. Before a nontitle fight in 1946 with Jackie Graves, he told sportswriter Don Riley, "I won't throw a punch in the third round. See how I come out." In the third round, Pep feinted and ducked, tripping up Graves so badly that the judges were completely unaware that Pep had not punched him once, and they awarded Pep the round. Five rounds later he knocked Graves out.

Pep, a native of Middletown, Connecticut, entered the ring at an early age, winning his state's flyweight and bantamweight championships when he was only a teenager. He turned pro soon after, fighting his first match in 1940 against James McGovern and winning it in four rounds. Pep went undefeated for the next sixty-one matches. He won the world featherweight title in 1942 over Chalky Wright and held the title through six defense matches, including a victory that he won less than a year after his legs were badly injured in a plane crash. The doctors had said that he would never fight again.

On October 29, 1948, Pep lost the title. His opponent, Sandy Saddler, was a tall, thin, and fast man who had a reputation for hitting hard and fighting dirty. Saddler absolutely destroyed Pep, who was unused to such vicious fighting. The match was stopped in the fourth round with the win going to Saddler. They fought again that February in Madison Square Garden, and this time Pep was ready. He outfooted and outboxed Saddler, regaining the title in a fifteen-round decision despite receiving two nasty cuts under his eyes that required eleven stitches to close.

Pep held on to the title until September 8, 1950, when he again faced his archenemy Saddler. In this match Saddler came out swinging and knocked Pep down in the third round, eventually dislocating the smaller man's shoulder in the seventh. Pep was forced to quit and Saddler again won the title. A year later, on September 26, 1951, Pep and Saddler had their last and most vicious fight. Pep, frustrated by Saddler's dirty tactics, decided to respond in kind. The two fighters used every illegal move possible, thumbing, wrestling, and butting each other in the ring until the severely beaten Pep was forced to retire in the tenth round. After the fight, the New York State Athletic Club revoked Pep's license and placed Saddler on suspension. Although Pep continued to box and win for many years after the famous Saddler match, he never got another chance at the featherweight title.

Pep boxed until 1959, when he announced his retirement after a ten-round decision loss to Sonny Leon. In 1965 he came out of retirement for a year and won every match until a six-round loss to Calvin Woodland in March 1966. He officially retired at age forty-three with a record of 230 wins, eleven losses, and only one draw. Willie Pep was elected into the Boxing Hall of Fame in 1990.

Of every professional heavyweight that has entered the ring, only one has walked away without suffering a single career loss. Rocky Marciano, born Rocco Francis Marchegiano, defeated forty-nine consecutive opponents with forty-three knockouts and retired having won every fight. As a teenager in Brockton, Massachusetts, Marciano played baseball for his high school, and he eventually gained a reputation as a home-run slugger and an especially proficient catcher. Marciano, however, threw out his arm and was moved to the outfield.

Later cut from the team, the disheartened Marciano dropped out of high school and sought work in the city. His father, Pierino Marchegiano, suffered great prejudice in his job as a shoe manufacturing plant worker and forbade his son to follow him into the profession, but Marciano, unable to hold a job elsewhere, eventually joined his father's plant. Though Marciano found his job as a

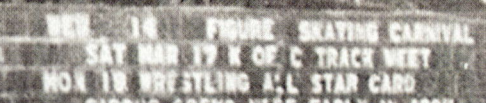

Left, above: Jake LaMotta was middleweight boxing champion of the world in 1949.

Left, below: Boxer Carmen Basilio was middleweight champion in 1957.

Right, above: Boxer Willie Pep—originally Guglielmo Papaleo—turned professional at age seventeen. After winning fifty-three consecutive fights, he beat Chalky Wright for the featherweight championship of the world.

Right: Boxer Rocky Graziano was middleweight champion of the world in 1974.

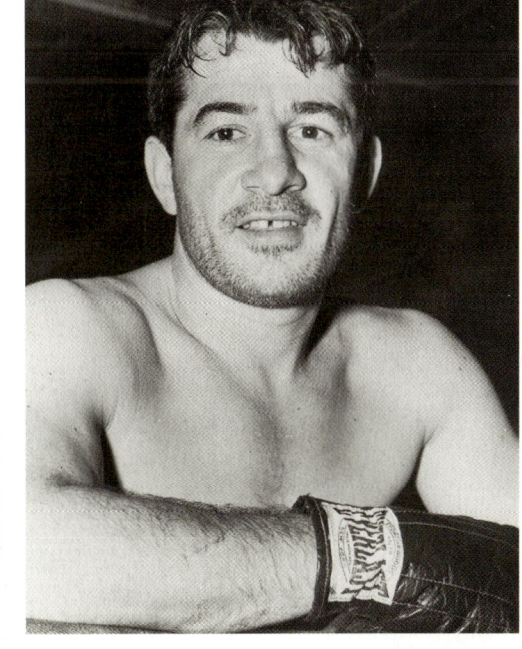

"shoe puller" tedious and boring, it did give him the opportunity to build his upper body and arms, which would figure prominently in his later success as a boxer.

Marciano's career at the plant did not last. He quickly developed an allergic reaction to leather dust and suffered from several bouts of claustrophobia. After quitting the shoe business, the twenty-year-old Marciano joined the army and was shipped to Ft. Lewis, where he took up amateur boxing. His first real fight was against Henry Lester, a former Golden Gloves champion. Marciano, despite his lack of training, did well enough against his seasoned opponent but was disqualified after he kneed Lester in the groin. In 1946 Marciano finished his tour of duty with the army and immediately focused all of his attention on baseball. Scouts noticed him, and they invited him to attend the annual Chicago Cubs tryouts that spring. Marciano's injured throwing arm plagued his performance and, told that he would never be a professional ballplayer, Marciano was cut from the team.

Rather than return to the shoe factory, Marciano decided to become a professional boxer instead. Because his mother hated the sport and refused to let him participate, Marciano and his trainer, Allie Colombo, trained in secret. They ran through the streets of Brockton almost every day while passing a football back and forth. This served a double purpose; while it fooled his mother, it also developed Marciano's arm and dramatically increased his punching accuracy. This helped Marciano's style tremendously. He had one of the shortest reaches of all the heavyweights, and often had to hurl himself at opponents to just make his punches connect. While he was not the most technically impressive boxer, Marciano could hit hard and hit often, softening up even the toughest opponent.

Marciano entered the professional ring to great drama on July 12, 1948, when he fought Harry Bilazarian in Providence, Rhode Island. The fight was over in minutes, with Marciano scoring a kayo on Bilazarian in the first round. Marciano knocked out his opponents in his next fourteen matches, and did so

Above: Champion swimmer and Olympic medalist Matt Biondi has set four world records. His eleven Olympic medals tie him with Mark Spitz as the most decorated U.S. Olympian in history.

Right: Skater Brian Boitano won an Olympic gold medal in 1988. Prior to that, he was a three-time winner of the men's singles in the World Figure Skating Championships.

SPORTS
155

At age fifteen, skater Linda Fratianne won the U.S. Ladies Figure Skating Championship. She was also winner of the 1977 and 1980 World Figure Skating Championships and of an Olympic silver medal in 1980. She was one of the few women skaters who could routinely execute triple jumps.

each time in fewer than six rounds. Quickly rising in the ranks, largely due to his insistence on fighting excellent boxers, Marciano eventually earned a match with his childhood hero, Joe Louis. In front of a stunned New York crowd, the youthful Marciano tore into Louis, pounding him repeatedly with his heavy guns. Marciano connected a vicious haymaker to Louis's head in the eighth round, and the former champion was down for the count. It was the third and last time Louis was ever defeated, and only the second time he had been kayoed. Marciano gained a shot a the title.

On September 23, 1952, Marciano fought Jersey Joe Walcott in Philadelphia for the World Heavyweight Championship. It was a grueling match from the start. Walcott knocked Marciano down in the first round and was ahead in points for the opening seven rounds. Finally, in the thirteenth round, Marciano dealt Walcott a terrific right cross, knocking him to the mat. The referee stopped the fight and Marciano was declared the winner and crowned the new world champion.

The "Brockton Blockbuster" defended his title six times, winning five of the matches by knockout. His last match was on September 21, 1955, a ninth-round knockout over Archie Moore. Less than a year later he announced his retirement, thus ending a brilliant and untarnished career. Tragically, Marciano died in a plane crash on August 31, 1969. He was only forty-six years old.

The middle of twentieth century ushered forth the golden age of middleweight boxing. Boxers such as Tony Zale, Marcel Cerdan, and the greatest, "Sugar" Ray Robinson, dominated the ring, and their fights were often the focus of the sports world. It was during this golden age that two of the greatest Italian-American middleweight boxers, Rocky Graziano and Jake LaMotta, were crowned champions.

Rocky Graziano was the first of the two boxers to win the title. Rising from the Italian ghettos of New York, Graziano overcame a troubled childhood to enter the professional ring. In his first match, on March 31, 1942, he floored

Hockey legend Phil Esposito was inducted into the Hockey Hall of Fame in 1984. A top NHL scorer, Esposito was also general manager of the New York Rangers.

Above: Jockey Eddie Arcaro was a five-time Kentucky Derby winner.

Right: Mario Andretti is congratulated on breaking the Indianapolis Speedway record, 1966. He went on to win the 1978 Grand Prix and had several victories at Daytona.

opponent Curtis Hightower in the second round. He went on to win forty-two of his next fifty-three matches. On September 27, 1946, Graziano fought his first title match against world middleweight champion Tony Zale. Both were excellent fighters, and for the first few rounds they were evenly matched. As the fight wore on, both men seemed to wear out. Suddenly, in the sixth round, the staggering Zale regained his composure long enough to belt Graziano hard in the stomach. Graziano fell to the floor and tried to rise, but Zale hit him again. Graziano crumpled to the mat and could not get back up before the referee called the count.

Zale and Graziano met again a year later in Chicago Stadium. Both men ripped into each other from the first round, with Graziano receiving a slash above one eye and a blinding hit to the other. Zale fared worse, however. The fight was stopped in the sixth round with Zale leaning hopelessly against the ropes. Graziano was declared the new middleweight champion of the world. The honor would not last, though. Zale regained the title a year later in a disappointing third-round knockout over Graziano. Graziano had one more shot at the title on April 16, 1952, when he fought "Sugar Ray" Robinson. Graziano was unable to wrest the title away from him. He later retired with a career record of 67-10-6, with fifty-two knockouts.

After his last match in 1952, Graziano entered show business, enjoying great success as a guest star on the Martha Raye show. The audience loved his thick New York accent and colorful sense of humor so much that he was invited to stay on the show for several weeks. Later his autobiography, *Somebody Up There Likes Me,* was adapted into a movie that won him even greater celebrity status.

Jake LaMotta, another of New York's sons and a childhood friend of Graziano, survived a troubled and violent youth to develop into one of the most punishing, and punished, middleweight champions ever. LaMotta, born Giacobe LaMotta, discovered boxing while serving time in a center for juvenile delinquents. When he was released, LaMotta turned away from crime and put all of

SPORTS
159

his effort toward boxing. Gaining professional status, LaMotta fought his first match on March 3, 1941, against Charley Mackley. He won the match in four rounds.

After tearing through the middleweight division for more than a year, LaMotta finally met his match on October 2, 1942, when he boxed against Sugar Ray Robinson for the first time. The match was brutal, but Robinson proved too quick and tough for the Bronx Bull, and he won in a ten-round decision. They fought again the following year, on February 5, and this time LaMotta gave Robinson his all, at one point knocking him right through the ropes. The match ended in the tenth round with LaMotta winning the decision. It was Sugar Ray

Bruno Sammartino, a professional wrestler, became the world champion in 1963 and held on to that title for twelve years.

Robinson's first professional loss, and indeed his last for many more years.

LaMotta had four more fights against Robinson, and lost all of them. The last match was one of the most brutal and one-sided matches in boxing history. On February 14, 1951, LaMotta, who had starved himself to meet the weight requirement, was virtually torn to shreds by a fresher and more prepared Robinson. By the end of the thirteenth round, the broken and defenseless LaMotta had only the ring ropes to hold him up while he endured a savage beating to his face and head. The Bronx Bull, however, refused to surrender. When the referee finally ended the fight with a technical knockout going to Robinson, LaMotta still had not gone down. The whole episode was dubbed the St. Valentine's Day Massacre by the sports press. LaMotta, however, was one of the few opponents whom Robinson was unable to knock down, an impressive feat considering that they had fought together six times. *The Ring* magazine later recognized him as the fighter with the all-time "toughest chin."

After years of winning matches against tough opponents, LaMotta finally got a chance at the world middleweight title. He fought reigning champion Marcel Cerdan on June 16, 1949, and beat him with a decisive tenth-round knockout. LaMotta defended his title a year later in a match against Laurent Dauthuille that *The Ring* later named Fight of the Decade and Greatest Come-From-Behind Victory. Finding himself too far behind in points to win by decision, LaMotta continued to play the part of the beaten champion in the final round by letting his opponent push him around the ring. Suddenly, with the match drawing to a close, LaMotta swung a massive left hook that caught the unsuspecting Dauthuille full on the jaw. Dauthuille sagged backward and Lamotta issued a barrage of punches, knocking out his opponent with only thirteen seconds left in the round.

When LaMotta retired from boxing on June 2, 1954, he had amassed a lifetime record of 83–19–4 with thirty knockouts. After falling into obscurity for many years, LaMotta once again rose to stardom when Martin Scorsese and Robert DeNiro approached him proposing a movie based on LaMotta's tell-all biography, *Raging Bull*. LaMotta agreed, and the film was released in 1980 to widespread public and critical acclaim. DeNiro won the Academy Award for Best Actor that year for his gripping portrayal of LaMotta, and the film was later named by several critics as the "Film of the Decade." Today, the long-retired

LaMotta spends many of his evenings as a comic entertainer, delighting audiences with his humorous anecdotes and jokes.

Carmen Basilio held titles in not one but two weight classes. The son of a poor onion farmer, Basilio fought his way to world renown by winning both the welterweight and the middleweight championships. His first professional match was on November 24, 1948, against Jimmy Evans. The fight ended when he kayoed Evans in the third round. Basilio continued to win most of his fights for the next several years.

While Basilio did not possess a lot of natural boxing talent, he won many of his victories by sheer virtue of his enormous courage and relentless punching. This courage propelled Basilio to his first welterweight championship match on September 18, 1953. Basilio lost to Kid Gavilan in a fifteen-round decision in that match, but got another chance at the title on June 10, 1955, against Tony DeMarco. He knocked out DeMarco in the twelfth round to secure the championship. He fought DeMarco again in November in a title rematch and again knocked him out in twelve rounds. The following year, Basilio lost the title to Johnny Saxton in a controversial decision but won it back in a ninth-round kayo against Saxton seven months later.

In 1957 Basilio moved up a weight class to compete for the middleweight title. He fought Sugar Ray Robinson for the championship at Yankee Stadium on September 23 and barely held on to a lead over his aging opponent to win in a split decision. In the rematch, held a year later on March 25 in Chicago Stadium, Robinson cut Basilio's eye in the early rounds so that it swelled completely shut. Even half-blinded, Basilio continued to dig into Robinson, but the cut had done its damage and Basilio ultimately lost the match and the title in a fifteen-round split decision.

Basilio retired in 1961 with a career record of 56–16–7 and twenty-seven knockouts. With his retirement, boxing had lost one of its hardest workers and biggest crowd-pleasers. Basilio was inducted into the International Boxing Hall of Fame in 1990.

Before he turned pro, Ray "Boom Boom" Mancini, a native of Youngstown, Ohio, first won several amateur tournaments, including the Golden Gloves. His two-fisted fighting style was a throwback to his father, Lenny, who had inspired him to put on the gloves. Mancini's first professional match was on October 18,

1979, when he won over Phil Bowen with an explosive first-round kayo. Mancini continued to win, beating his next nineteen opponents before being stopped by Alexis Arguello in the fourteenth round of the WBA lightweight championship.

In 1982 Mancini finally won the WBA lightweight title with a sudden first-round knockout of reigning champion Arturo Frias. Mancini held on to the championship for two years. He concluded his career with a record of 25–5, with twenty-three kayos.

Angelo Merena, a.k.a. Angelo Dundee, is credited with managing and training fifteen world champions. His most famous contender was Cassius Clay, the controversial champion who later changed his name to Muhammad Ali. He also handled other champs, including Carmen Basilio and Sugar Ray Leonard, and is revered as the greatest trainer in boxing history. Another premier trainer is Lou Duva. He began his career as a bucket boy, and within the next fifty years became the sport's top manager and trainer, working more than eighty world-title fights. Duva also has fifteen champions to his credit, including Pernell Whitaker and Evander Holyfield. He was voted manager of the year by the Boxing Writers Association of America in 1985 and the World Boxing Association's trainer of the year in 1987. Duva was inducted into the International Boxing Hall of Fame in 1997.

Willie Mosconi was world billiards champion during the 1940s and 1950s.

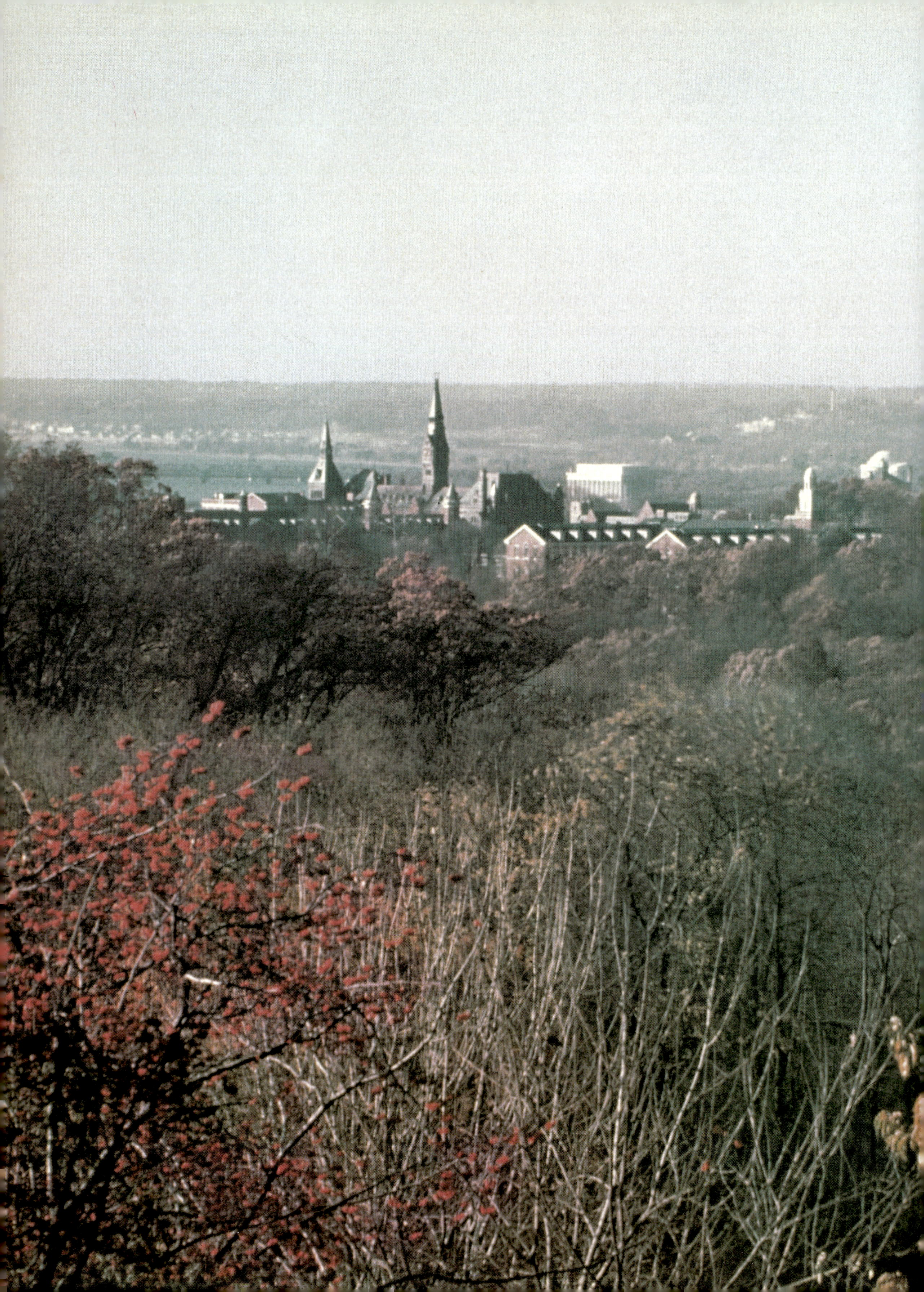

EDUCATION, SCIENCE, AND MEDICINE

Advances in education, science, and medicine help determine the degree of evolution of a civilization. Every goal attained in these fields bestows on a country prestige, international credibility, and authority.

The history of Italians in the United States includes personal and professional vicissitudes. Italian Americans were initially hindered by discrimination against immigrants, by a low level of education, and by a tendency to isolate themselves in their own ethnicity. Over time, however, a remarkable number of scientists, doctors, and teachers with Italian last names have contributed to research, experimentation, university culture, and scientific discoveries in this country.

For two primary reasons, this is not surprising. First, Italy is a country historically well developed in these fields. Italian scientists and educators in the fifteenth century were already earning respect and praise all over the world for their pioneering research and contributions to social development. Second, the Italians in the United States, even the ones coming from the lowest social ranks, have had an extraordinary ability to overcome adversity.

EDUCATIONAL ACHIEVEMENTS

From the period of early immigration in the late 1800s to the present day, Italian Americans have made remarkable advances in educational achievement. Not only has attendance by students at all levels of education increased over the years, but significant numbers of Italian Americans have entered the teaching profession.

View of Georgetown University, Washington, D.C.

Italian genius Leonardo da Vinci, an inspiration in art and invention.

As discussed earlier, often Italian immigrants did not consider education as a means to improve their standard of living. As a result they sent their children to menial jobs instead of school. When the government passed legislation in the 1930s to stop child labor, a dramatic upsurge in school attendance occurred among Italian immigrant families.

Furthermore, a growing availability of white-collar work for high school graduates made education more appealing to Italian Americans who saw it as a means to finding better jobs. By that time, a number of Italian immigrants had become teachers, principals, and educational leaders who used their talents to promote and improve education in the United States not only for other Italian Americans but for all Americans. Outstanding among these educators was Leonard Covello who taught in New York City's Harlem and changed the lives of thousands of Italian- and Spanish-American students during his long career from the 1920s to the 1950s.

Long before the first wave of Italian immigrants hit these shores, however, Italians played a role in developing U.S. education. Some of the most passionate promoters of education were Roman Catholic clergy—the Jesuits and Franciscans in particular. Starting with little means and few students, they created schools and universities that have become strong and prestigious institutions.

Among the Jesuits who have contributed the most to the founding of schools are John Nobili and A. Accolti, who founded the University of Santa Clara in California in 1851; Joseph Cataldo, who helped establish in 1881 what today is Gonzaga University in Washington state; and Father Pamphilus, who founded St. Bonaventure University in New York State in 1858.

Catholic clergy also became presidents of respected U.S. universities at the beginning of the nineteenth century. Among them were Giovanni Grassi, who took office as president of Georgetown University in 1812, only two years after emigrating from Bergamo; Anthony Ciampi, who became president of Loyola College in Baltimore in 1863; and Lawrence B. Palladino, president of Gonzaga University from 1894 to 1897.

In 1889, Frances Cabrini, an Italian nun, was sent by Pope Leo XIII as a missionary to help Italian immigrants in the United States. Endowed with strong faith and a constructive spirit, Mother Cabrini, who became a U.S. citizen in 1909, helped establish fourteen American colleges, ninety-eight schools, twenty-eight

EDUCATION, SCIENCE, AND MEDICINE

167

EDUCATION, SCIENCE, AND MEDICINE

168

DIALOGO
di
GALILEO GALILEI LINCEO
AL SER.mo FERD. II. GRAN. DVCA DI
TOSCANA

Stefan. Della Be

orphanages, eight hospitals, three training schools, and the Missionary Sisters of the Sacred Heart, an order consisting of more than four thousand sisters recruited to help her in her mission. Because of her dedication to helping others in such an expansive manner, Mother Cabrini was canonized in 1946, becoming the first American saint.

Among the founders and presidents of institutions and universities, Peter Sammartino and his wife, Sally Scaramelli, stand out. In 1942 they founded Fairleigh Dickinson University in Rutherford, New Jersey, a liberal arts institution that grew over the years to become America's eighth-largest privately supported university.

Another outstanding educator was Angelo Bartlett Giamatti, who was not only admired in the field of higher education but also remembered for his passion for baseball. He was named president of Yale University in 1978, becoming the first Italian American ever to hold the post and, at forty, the youngest president in that Ivy League school's long history. In 1989 he left Yale to become the commissioner of Major League Baseball.

In the nineteenth and twentieth centuries, Italian-American educators such as Francesco De Vico, Angelo Secchi, Pietro Bachi, Vincenzo Botta, Charles Constantine Pise, and Camillus Mazzella taught at Georgetown University, Mount St. Mary's College, Harvard University, and New York University. In 1998 the National Italian American Foundation in Washington, D.C., identified at least 166 college presidents of Italian descent.

Proving that learning can occur outside of the classroom as well as within, a number of Italian

Left: Frontispiece of a book by Galileo, showing Aristotle, Ptolemy, and Copernicus discussing astronomy, published in 1632.

Above: The title page from Galileo's *Discorsi e Dimostrazioni Matematiche*, published 1638.

EDUCATION, SCIENCE, AND MEDICINE

Left: Mother Frances Cabrini, the first American saint, founded colleges, hospitals, and other institutions with the help of the Missionary Sisters of the Sacred Heart. She died in 1917 and was canonized in 1946.

Right: His eminence Anthony Cardinal Bevilacqua, Archbishop of Philadelphia.

Americans have launched programs that assist schools in imaginative ways. In 1985 Linda Lantieri co-founded Resolving Conflicts Creatively, an organization in New York City that teaches students how to prevent violence in the classroom, resolve their differences, and develop friendships.

In 1987 Matilda Cuomo, wife of the former New York governor, Mario Cuomo, founded Mentoring USA, a program launched in New York State to give children role models through a one-on-one mentoring program in the state's schools. The program has been adopted by at least eight other states and in Italy, and assists more than ten thousand children.

Rosemarie Truglio is the director of research for "Sesame Street", the award-winning PBS children's program, where she works to enhance the program's educational and entertainment values.

Increases in Italian-American attendance and achievement in education continue as studies show that more and more Italian-American men and women are seeking higher education and entering the professional workforce. Statistics from the 1990 Census reveal that, of the six million Italian Americans in the U.S. labor force, fully two-thirds are employed in white-collar positions.

SCIENCE

The achievements of Italian scientists from the Middle Ages to the present day are universally recognized. In addition to painting and sculpting, Leonardo da Vinci investigated problems in geology, botany, hydraulics, and mechanics in the fifteenth century. In the sixteenth and seventeenth centuries, Galileo Galilei overturned previously held beliefs with his pioneering discoveries and theories; scientists such as biologists Morgagni, Malpighi, and Frascaturo and physicists Porta, Santorio, and Torricelli all contributed groundbreaking work to their fields.

During the nineteenth and twentieth centuries, a number of Italian scientists and inventors left Italy to pursue scientific studies in the United States. Antonio Meucci is credited with the idea of the first telephone in Italy in 1849, twenty-seven years before Alexander Graham Bell patented his invention. When he immigrated to the United States in 1850, Meucci attempted to secure a patent, but could not afford the fees. Bell's presentation of his early model of the telephone turned into a lengthy legal ordeal that ended with the attribution of the invention to the American. Without underestimating the scientific value of Bell's work and without putting history on trial, it is justified to hypothesize that if Meucci had been able to patent his creation at the moment of its conception, the invention of the telephone might today be attributed to an Italian.

Gaetano Lanza, born in 1848 to Sicilian immigrants in the United States, became the founder of the engineering department at the Massachusetts Institute of Technology. In 1909 Lanza's work as an inventor resulted in the creation of the first wind tunnel, which was used to test aerodynamic effects.

The man who directed the *Apollo 11* launch operations, oversaw the first lunar landing, and helped make possible the first moon walk in 1969 was another Italian American, Rocco Petrone.

Albert Sacco, Jr., born in Boston, was aboard the space shuttle *Columbia* in 1995 as a payload specialist. He spent sixteen days in space within the pressurized Spacelab module studying biotechnology, combustion science, and fluid physics. Sacco currently holds the George A. Snell Chair of Engineering and is the direc-

EDUCATION, SCIENCE, AND MEDICINE

172

Guglielmo Marconi, right, used a radio transmitter onboard the yacht *Electra*, left, to light lamps eleven thousand miles away in Sydney, Australia, circa 1920–1930.

tor of the Center for Advanced Microgravity Materials Processing at Northeastern University in Boston.

THE NOBEL PRIZE

The greatest international recognition of achievement in the sciences and medicine is undoubtedly the Nobel Prize. Ten Italians and Italian Americans to date have received this prestigious prize for their outstanding accomplishments in physics, physiology, and chemistry.

The 1909 Nobel Prize in physics was awarded to the Italian Guglielmo Marchese Marconi for his development of wireless telegraphy. He invented a practical antenna and succeeded in sending signals over a distance of more than one mile.

In 1938 the Italian-born scientist Enrico Fermi was awarded the Nobel Prize in physics for his work on radioactive substances. Fermi and his wife, who was Jewish, chose not to return to Fascist Italy on their way back from Stockholm after receiving the prize. Instead they moved to the United States. Fermi discovered element 93, neptunium, by bombarding uranium in an attempt to produce an element of a higher atomic number, and in 1942 he created the first self-sustaining chain reaction in uranium. His research preceded his active participation in the atomic bomb project alongside other Italian Americans including Alfonso Tammaro, Joseph T. Gemmi, Armando Spadetti, and Albert Ghiorso.

The Nobel Prize in physics was awarded in 1959 to the Italian American Emilio Segrè. Deeply anti-Fascist, Segrè had left Italy for America in part because he was of Jewish as well as Christian heritage. He is credited with the discovery of the element astatine, the isotope plutonium-239, and the first artificially produced element, technetium. Other Nobel Prizes went to Riccardo Giacconi (1960), who, working with Italian-American scientists Bruno Rossi and Frank

The late Joseph Cardinal Bernardin, archbishop of Chicago, with Bill Clinton. He was appointed archbishop of Chicago in 1982 by Pope John Paul II, and has received numerous honorary doctorates and honors from colleges and universities throughout the world.

Paolini, succeeded in detecting X rays in space, and to Carlo Rubia (1984) for his work in subatomic particles.

Four other Italian Americans were awarded Nobel Prizes for their work in the sciences: Renato Dulbecco, Giulio Natta, Salvador Edward Luria, and Louis Ignarro. Dulbecco was born in Italy in 1914 and in 1947 moved to the United States, where he worked in various research facilities and universities as professor of pathology and medicine. In 1975 he was awarded the Nobel Prize in physiology by demonstrating that certain viruses can cause some cells to become cancerous. Natta received the Nobel Prize in chemistry in 1963 for his invention of a method of producing isostatic hydrocarbon polymers. Luria, born in Italy in 1912, worked as a biologist in the United States and was awarded the Nobel Prize in medicine in 1969 for his work in the field of bacterial viruses. And in 1998 Ignarro received the prestigious prize for his discovery of the physiological role of nitric oxide, which has many medical applications, including the production of Viagra.

Rita Levi-Montalcini was born in Italy in 1909, moved to the United States in 1947, and became a citizen in 1956. One of the first women to perform ground-breaking research on the nerve-growth factor, she received the Nobel Prize in 1986 for describing how tumors can affect a nerve's growth.

ITALIAN AMERICANS IN MEDICINE

One of the first Italian-American physicians was Felix Formento, who was chief surgeon of the Louisiana Confederate Hospital during the Civil War. In 1859, Tullio Suzzara Verdi became the first Italian immigrant to graduate from a U.S. medical school, Philadelphia's Hahnemann College. In 1865, Verdi assisted William Henry Seward, President Lincoln's secretary of state, when he was wounded as part of the assassination plot against Lincoln. Antonio Lagorio, who founded the Pasteur Institute in Chicago in 1890, was one of the first Italian Americans to earn both medical and legal degrees.

Starting in the 1930s, Vincent Ciccone received numerous patents for developing methods of mass-producing penicillin and for combining medicine with hard candy, a procedure that led to the creation of cough drops.

Edmund Pellegrino, a physician who now directs the Georgetown University Center for the Advanced Study of Ethics in Washington, D.C., Is a pioneer in the field of medical ethics in the United States. Pellegrino has advocated that medical students receive early instruction in ethical principles to ensure that a physician's methods of treatment not only address the medical details of the patient's case but also consider the patient's personal values.

Louis Lasagna studied medical ethics from the perspective of clinical research. He became involved in drug regulation and development and founded the first academic group devoted to clinical pharmacology. He supported the use of placebo-controlled clinical trials in the 1960s, lobbied for faster approval of AIDS drugs in the 1980s, and in 1995 received the American Association for the Advancement of Science Lifetime Mentorship Award.

Most recently, Italian Americans have been at the forefront of the war against AIDS. Robert Gallo, the grandson of a Northern Italian immigrant, became interested in medicine during his childhood after his younger sister developed leukemia. He succeeded in identifying the T-cell viral cause of leukemia in 1978. Gallo's most renowned achievement came in 1984, when he codiscovered HIV, the virus associated with AIDS, with French scientist Luc Montagnier. He also developed the test that safeguards the world's blood supply against the disease, and holds or shares seventy-nine patents. His discoveries have generated more than $1 billion in private-sector revenues.

Anthony Fauci, M.D., is director of the National Institute of Allergy and Infectious Diseases in Maryland. He oversees the development of testing and therapies to help people with AIDS and other immunological illnesses.

Anthony Fauci is director of the National Institutes of Allergy and Infectious Diseases in Maryland and was formerly the director of the Office of AIDS Research. Fauci, once a staunch supporter of strict and thorough experimental drug testing, had a dramatic change of heart after meeting with an AIDS patient who faced losing his sight because he could not get an existing but unapproved drug that would save his vision without interfering with his AIDS reatment regimen. Fauci pushed the Food and Drug Administration for a "parallel track" of testing for AIDS drugs, which would allow wider access to therapies for patients who don't meet the rigorous criteria to qualify for the main track of traditional AIDS studies.

In the branch of neurosurgery, Leonard Cerullo

developed the use of lasers and founded the Chicago Institute of Neurosurgery and Neuroresearch in the 1980s. Antonio Gotto is cochairman of the United States–Italian Cardiovascular Working Group of the National Heart, Lung, and Blood Institute. One of the leaders in lipid research, his studies have offered compelling evidence that modifying serum cholesterol concentrations can reduce heart attacks and slow the progression of arteriosclerotic disease.

Several women have appeared prominently in the history of Italian Americans' contributions to medicine. In 1899 Annina Carmilla Rondinella was the first Italian-American woman on record to receive a U.S. medical degree. Half a century later, Margaret Giannini dedicated her life to working with the handicapped and the physically disabled. While her initial focus was on children, Giannini later extended her studies to adults, and in 1950 she founded and became director of the Mental Retardation Institute in New York. To this day, the institute, which began as a small clinic, remains the world's largest facility for the physically and mentally handicapped.

And in 2000 Catherine De Angelis became the first woman editor of the *Journal of the American Medical Association* in its 116-year-history.

Italian Americans have come a long way since the days when education was a luxury. Their recent successes in science and medicine have required rigorous and demanding academic training. Today doctors, scientists, and researchers of Italian heritage represent a significant presence in their fields.

"Father Dag," Angelo D'Agostino, with a young orphan in Kenya. Father D'Agostino runs an orphanage that cares for children with AIDS. The son of Italian immigrants, he practiced medicine in Washington, D.C., until 1966 when he became a Jesuit. In 1986 he went to Kenya and founded the Nairobi orphanage in 1992.

EDUCATION,
SCIENCE,
AND MEDICINE

177

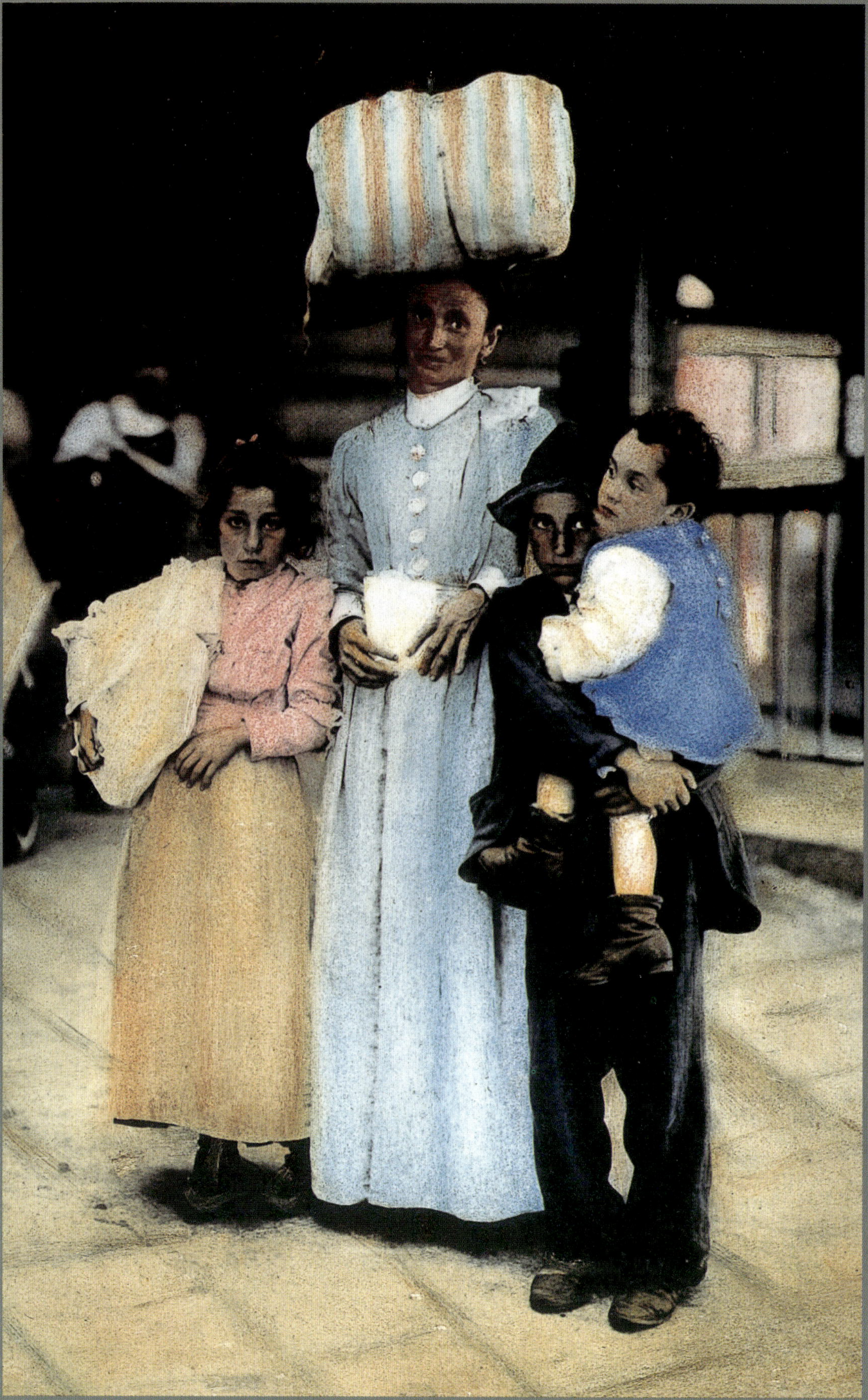

ITALIAN-AMERICAN WOMEN

◆

YESTERDAY, TODAY, AND TOMORROW

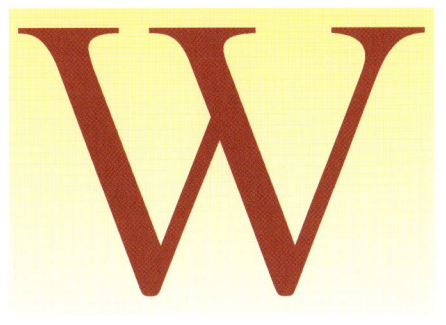

What does it mean to be an Italian-American woman at the dawn of a new century? The question is harder to answer than it would seem. Most people would agree that being a woman in the United States today is far more complicated than it used to be.

Never before in our history has a woman had so many opportunities to get an education, embark on a career, and become a leader in her community. But with these golden opportunities comes the more traditional expectation that she will also marry and have children. In other words, American society tells women they can have it all, but expects them to *do* it all as well.

While many women today struggle to balance these opportunities and responsibilities, Italian-American women have it a little tougher than the rest because their heritage places an extraordinary emphasis on the family and on the woman's role in that family. *"Casa senza donna, barca senza timone"*—a house without a woman is like a ship without a rudder, our grandparents used to say. The proverb underscores the crucial role that women play in creating and preserving a family. So what does an Italian-American woman do to realize her full potential?

The first generation of Italian women in the United States would not have had a problem answering that question. For them, realizing their potential and taking care of their families were one and the same. Most came over during the Great Migration of the late nineteenth and early twentieth centuries that brought an estimated five million Italians to these shores. They came with their

Italian immigrant family, c. 1910.

fathers, brothers, and husbands, and some brave souls even came alone as mail-order brides.

For them, being an Italian-American woman meant being a good wife and mother. The family was the center of their lives, and their own desires were sacrificed to it. So they comforted their husbands and children in a new land and prided themselves on their spotless kitchens and homemade pasta, their starched white sheets and frugal housekeeping. They also worked outside the home as seamstresses in sweatshops or behind the counters in their husbands' stores. But their jobs were not careers. They worked to help the family survive.

The daughters these women raised were Italian-American women of a new generation. Unlike their mothers, they spoke fluent English and had high-school educations. After they graduated they found office jobs, and when they married they had fewer children. But with motherhood their lives became more traditional. Often they would quit their jobs to devote themselves to their families. They were *"tutta casa e chiesa"*—all home and church, the traditional and idealized Italian (and Italian-American) wife and mother.

Isn't it strange, then, that they did not raise their daughters to follow in their footsteps? They sent their girls to college instead of into the kitchen. Secretly, however, they packed their daughters' spiritual suitcases with the family heirlooms handed down from generation to generation of Italian-American women: the strength and courage that helped them cross an ocean and live in a strange new world; the loyalty and devotion to the family that helped them weather life's storms; and the fierce protective love for children that enabled them to sacrifice their own dreams to help their sons and daughters realize theirs.

Now these women are juggling the responsibilities of careers, marriage, and family. And they, too, have daughters—the fourth generation of Italian-American women—whose turn it is to carry the suitcase of family heirlooms into a new century. Sometimes that suitcase will seem very heavy, but there is nothing in it that most Italian-American women would choose to discard. And they, like their mothers, grandmothers, and great-grandmothers, will find the strength to lift it.

We have come to rely on the legendary strength of our Italian-American women. We've even idealized it, as Susan Caperna Lloyd observes in her excellent and moving book *No Pictures in My Grave*. The book begins with a scene from her Italian-American grandmother's funeral. As he stood at his mother's coffin, her

A family shells nuts for a living in a New York tenement, circa 1911. The mother nurses a baby while she works with the other children, Rosie, Genevieve, and Tessie.

father took a picture of himself and his son out of his wallet and put it in his dead mother's hands. "This way she'll pray for us," he told his daughter. And Lloyd thought, "Not even death could destroy in my father's mind his belief in the power of his mother to protect her family even from beyond the grave."

THE FIRST GENERATION

In the immigration saga of the millions of Italians who arrived on American shores, it was often the women who had the most demanding and difficult roles. Most of them came from Southern Italy, where social norms and a feudal society had for centuries excluded them from life outside the home. Once they arrived in the United States, however, Italian women found themselves faced with the enormous challenge of making their time-honored values, which made the family the nucleus of society and its strongest foundation, compatible with the ideas of personal freedom and individualism upon which the United States was built.

Taking care of the family's most basic needs for food and shelter was so difficult for these early immigrants that every member of the family, including the women, had to work. For the first time in their lives, many Italian wives and daughters had to find income-producing work to help support the family. At the beginning, most worked at home, often making artificial flowers, sewing clothing, packaging tobacco, or taking in boarders.

Before long, however, women began leaving their cottage industries to work in factories, especially in the burgeoning textile trades of the northeastern cities, where they worked in the infamous sweatshops. Their entrance into the working world was hard and at times traumatic thanks to working conditions that included long hours, poorly lit and ventilated factories, and among the lowest wages in the U.S. labor market. Among the hundreds of thousands of Italian women who came to the United States in the late nineteenth century were two who were destined to make a difference in the lives of underprivileged people all over the country.

Both were Catholic nuns who came to the United States as missionaries. Sister Blandina Segale arrived in the closing decades of the nineteenth century and traveled to the Southwest. In 1881 she founded the first public school in New Mexico, and in 1893 she became the first Italian-American woman author ever to be published. Her book, *At the End of the Santa Fe Trail,* recounts her life and ordeals as a religious worker among the people of New Mexico.

Mother Frances Cabrini came to the United States in 1889 and became a U.S. citizen in 1909. During transatlantic voyages between Italy and the United States, she observed the immigration phenomenon firsthand and came to understand the enormous hardships these families bore. On the ships, she saw people crowded together, living in the poorest sanitary conditions. She did her best to help those who fell ill during the journey, especially the children.

In New York City and later in Chicago, Mother Cabrini continued her charitable work with Italian immigrant families who were struggling to overcome difficult living conditions. With the help of the religious order she had founded, the Missionary Sisters of the Sacred Heart, the Italian nun succeeded in tasks that seemed impossible. She helped the men get jobs, found food and clothing for the children and encouraged them to go to school, and comforted the women, who were homesick for their familiar faith, traditions, and beliefs.

The accomplishments of Mother Cabrini and her army of four thousand faithful nuns include the founding of ninety-eight schools, fourteen colleges, twenty-eight orphanages, eight hospitals, and three training schools. Under her direction, the Missionary Sisters of the Sacred Heart traveled to the largest cities of the United States, helping the needy of all races and creeds as well as her Italian compatriots transplanted in a new land.

Although Mother Cabrini suffered from delicate health all her life, she carried out great projects. Her charitable work touched so many that after her death in 1917 she was canonized, becoming America's first saint in 1946.

EARLY STRUGGLES

Mother Cabrini's efforts notwithstanding, Italian immigrant women still had heavy burdens to bear. Part of the problem was that they were largely unskilled and poorly educated. At first they found work in textile factories. The language barrier prevented them from moving up to better jobs, so they earned little and endured terrible working conditions that were often dangerous as well.

In Manhattan, for example, the Triangle Shirtwaist Company fire of 1911 claimed the lives of nearly 150 women, most of them Italian and Jewish immigrants. Many women died because the emergency exits were blocked, the elevators broken, and the fire escapes in poor condition.

Coffins of the victims—many of them young Italian women and girls—after the Triangle Shirtwaist Company fire in 1911.

Until the 1920s, Italian-American women workers were not unionized, but tragedies such as the Triangle Shirtwaist Company fire, coupled with low-paying jobs, encouraged these women to organize to achieve at least minimally safe working conditions and better salaries.

By 1910, more than 35 percent of Italian women in the workforce were in the needle trades. In 1917 Angela Bambace, an enterprising eighteen-year-old New Yorker, tried to organize the workers in the East Harlem shirtwaist factory where she and her sister, Maria, were employed. A constant figure at the rallies the two sister held was their mother, armed with a rolling pin to protect her activist daughters.

The union that the Bambace sisters supported was the International Ladies' Garment Workers' Union (ILGWU). At that time, however, the ILGWU was dominated by Jewish leaders, who frequently excluded Italians not only from elected posts but also from membership in certain locals. Italians began demanding union locals of their own. In 1919 they established one such local, number 89, for dressmakers. Most dressmakers were women, but Local 89's leadership was dominated by men.

Angela and Maria Bambace helped organize the 1919 garment workers' strikes that led to the founding of Local 89. Angela worked for the ILGWU for the rest of her life, eventually becoming vice president of the union. She was the first Italian-American woman ever to hold an executive position in the union's history.

Two other women of Italian descent also were prominent in America's early labor movement: Margaret DiMaggio and Tina Catania. Like Bambace, they became leaders in the ILGWU and Local 89. DiMaggio convinced many Italian women to join the union and even went to jail several times for her union activities. Later, in the 1930s, she became an ardent New Deal supporter who worked with Eleanor Roosevelt on many issues and even spoke at the White House. By the time she retired, DiMaggio held the position of assistant manager of ILGWU's organization department. By the mid-1930s, thanks to the efforts of the Bambace sisters, DiMaggio, and other Italian-American women, New York's Italian dressmakers' Local 89 had more than forty thousand members and was the largest union local in the country.

These women were part of the burgeoning American labor movement that grew stronger during the early decades of the twentieth century. Then as now, strikes were the most effective tools workers had to force employers to improve wages and working conditions. Strikes such as the one waged in 1913 by the 25,000 workers at the Paterson Silk Factory in New Jersey helped pave the way to the eight-hour workday, an end to child labor, and better wages. During the course of the six-month strike, Maria Botto and her husband, Pietro, opened their home in Haledon, New Jersey, to the demonstrators. Today their home is a national landmark and the official headquarters of the American Labor Museum.

While these women were making history in the labor movement, a young Italian-American woman, little more than a girl, was breaking new ground for American-born singers in the competitive and demanding world of grand opera. In 1918 Rosa Ponselle became the first U.S.-trained singer to perform at New

We Can Do It!
WESTINGHOUSE
POST FEB. 15 TO FEB. 28
WAR PRODUCTION CO-ORDINATING COMMITTEE

York's famed Metropolitan Opera. Born Rosa Ponzillo in Connecticut, she made her debut at the Met in Giuseppe Verdi's *La Forza del Destino* opposite Enrico Caruso.

Ponselle had been discovered singing with her sister in a vaudeville act. This young talent, dubbed the "Cinderella of Opera," went on to sing more than twenty roles in her nineteen-year career at the Met, and was one of the most glamorous stars in the company's galaxy. She retired in 1936 to marry and teach, and died in 1981 at age eighty-three, a true American success story.

THE NEXT GENERATION

Life slowly improved for the first generation of Italian women in the United States, and by the 1930s and 1940s their daughters began moving up the career ladder. Better educated and more at ease in American society, this next generation of Italian-American women shunned the factories and instead sought work in stores and businesses offices. Some even started their own businesses.

During the Depression, for example, Celeste Lizio, a young Italian woman, arrived in the United States and opened a restaurant in Chicago with her husband. Celeste went on to found Mama Celeste's Pizza, a line of frozen Italian foods that she eventually sold to Quaker Oats and which is today found in supermarket freezers all over the country.

Italian-American women also established themselves in professions usually reserved for men. At the beginning of the twentieth century, Mariana Bertola, for example, became one of the first woman physicians. An obstetrician, teacher, and political activist, she founded women's clubs and associations, becoming known in California as "Dr. Crusader." It is thanks to her efforts that every hospital in that state has a maternity ward and a pediatric ward.

A generation later, and on the other side of the country, another Italian-American woman physician became a a pioneer in helping the disabled. In 1950 Margaret J. Giannini founded the Mental Retardation Institute of New York City, the first and largest facility for the mentally handicapped in the world.

And in 2000, as the new century dawned, Catherine De Angelis, M.D., became the first woman editor in the 116-year-history of the prestigious *Journal of the American Medical Association*.

The achievements of women like these were an indication of the new level

This familiar poster proclaiming "We Can Do It" is of Rosie the Riveter, who was modeled on Rosie Bonavita of Long Island, New York. Rosie the Riveter represented the women who helped the American war effort by taking men's places in factories during World War II.

Gymnast Mary Lou Retton, born Mary Lou Rettoni, wins an Olympic gold medal in 1984.

of expectations set before Italian-American women. At home they learned from their mothers the importance of family. They knew they were expected to become wives and mothers, but that did not preclude them from acquiring an education and a career.

Like their mothers and grandmothers, this next generation of Italian-American women also faced the challenge of balancing family and career. Such a challenge might lead to inner conflicts and identity crises, but remarkably, Italian-American women have largely been able to embrace both their American and Italian values, and in the process, to forge a new identity as Italian-American women.

WORLD WAR II

The terrible war years were a watershed for Italian-American women. An estimated twelve million American men, at least 10 percent of them Italian Americans, were in the U.S. armed forces, most of them fighting abroad. Back home, in offices and factories, women were taking the place of their brothers, sons, husbands, and fathers to support their families and help the war effort.

The patriotic symbol of this modern American woman, fighting on the home front to protect her country, was Rosie the Riveter. Drawings of her, with her sleeves rolled up and a bandanna wrapped around her head to keep her hair out of the machinery, appeared on billboards and in magazines all over the country. The model who posed for this campaign was an Italian-American woman named Rosie Bonavita. "Rosie the Riveter" also was the title of a popular song of 1942 written about her by Rodd Evans and John J. Loeb. The next year, her image appeared on the cover of the *Saturday Evening Post* in a famous portrait by Norman Rockwell. After the war, Rosie Bonavita married James Hickey and lived in a Long Island suburb of New York City.

The postwar years also were a time when Italian Americans in general assumed a higher profile in American society. The patriotism and devotion they had shown during the war earned them the respect of the larger American public that their immigrant parents might have merited but did not enjoy. This new generation of Italian Americans, fluent in English and armed with high-school and university educations, was ready to become an integral part of American society.

COMING INTO THEIR OWN

An early indication of that sea-change in the status of Italian-American women appeared in the 1950 U.S. census. The statistics for that year revealed that 40 percent of Italian-American women held clerical or sales positions, compared to 8 percent of all women of foreign origin. Slowly, Italian-American women began to pursue more ambitious career goals than those of their mothers and grandmothers.

The 1960s and 1970s were a time of civil commitment and growing political awareness among Italian Americans. During those years, enterprising women of Italian descent created important activist associations. In 1964 Mary Sansone founded the Congress of Italian American Organizations (CIAO) with the aim of uniting the Italian-American community through civic activities.

Another important organization, the National Organization of Women (NOW), elected an Italian-American president, Eleanor Cutri Smeal, in 1970. Within two years, Smeal turned NOW into the largest women's organization in the world, with a total of 100,000 members. In 1980 Aileen Riotto Sirey founded the National Organization of Italian-American Women, the first such organization of its kind in the country.

TRAILBLAZERS

Italian-American women have an astonishing history of being the first woman in their fields. The first woman pilot in commercial airline history was Bonnie Tiburzi, hired in 1973 by American Airlines. The first American woman gymnast ever to bring

ITALIAN-
AMERICAN
WOMEN

190

home the Olympic gold medal was Mary Lou Retton, born Mary Lou Rettoni. The sixteen-year-old athlete won a record-breaking total of five medals in the 1984 Olympics in Los Angeles, becoming the youngest person in the U.S. Olympic Committee Hall of Fame.

In politics, the record of Italian-American women is equally impressive. In 1975 Ella Tambussi Grasso became the first woman in U.S. history ever to be elected governor in her own right. After having served in the U.S. House of Representatives, she was elected governor of Connecticut, the most powerful position ever obtained by a woman in politics at that time. Grasso's success offered proof that capable women could provide leadership at the highest levels of government.

Almost a decade later, in 1984, Geraldine Ferraro, a former U.S. congresswoman from New York, became the first woman ever to run for national office. Even though her bid for the vice presidency was unsuccessful, Ferraro's achievement revolutionized the political world, demonstrating that women can arrive at political heights usually reserved for men.

Among the women who wield considerable political power today are four Italian-American women serving in Congress: Rosa De Lauro, Constance Morella, Nancy Pelosi, and Marge Scafati Roukema. To this list we must add the businesswoman Patricia de Stacy Harrison. In 1997 she became the first person of Italian descent ever to be elected cochair of the Republican National Committee. Throughout her career as an author, businesswoman, and politician, de Stacy Harrison has helped women and minorities.

THE CHALLENGE TODAY

Italian-American women have come a long way since the time when the only place for a respectable woman was in the home. Today they move confidently through the world of work, their achievements notable in every sector from technology to publishing, from communications to the arts and entertainment, from fashion to business.

Often the American public does not know that these women are of Italian descent. Famed artist Georgia O'Keeffe, for example, was named for her Italian maternal grandfather, Giorgio Totto, who was born in Italy. And while people know that Oscar-winners Mira Sorvino and Marisa Tomei are of Italian descent,

Vice presidential candidate Geraldine Ferraro campaigns in San Francisco, California in 1984.

Left, above: Author Helen Barolini is one of the most prolific Italian-American writers. She has written essays, poems, literary criticism, and novels, including *Umbertina*, a multi-generational story of Italian-American women.

Right, above: Author Barbara Grizzuti Harrison, a talented, insightful writer. Her *Italian Days* is regarded as one of the best books about Italy.

Right: Sylvia Poggioli, NPR Correspondent, Foreign Desk (Italy).

Right: Mary Ann Esposito on the set of her cooking show for PBS, "Ciao Italia".

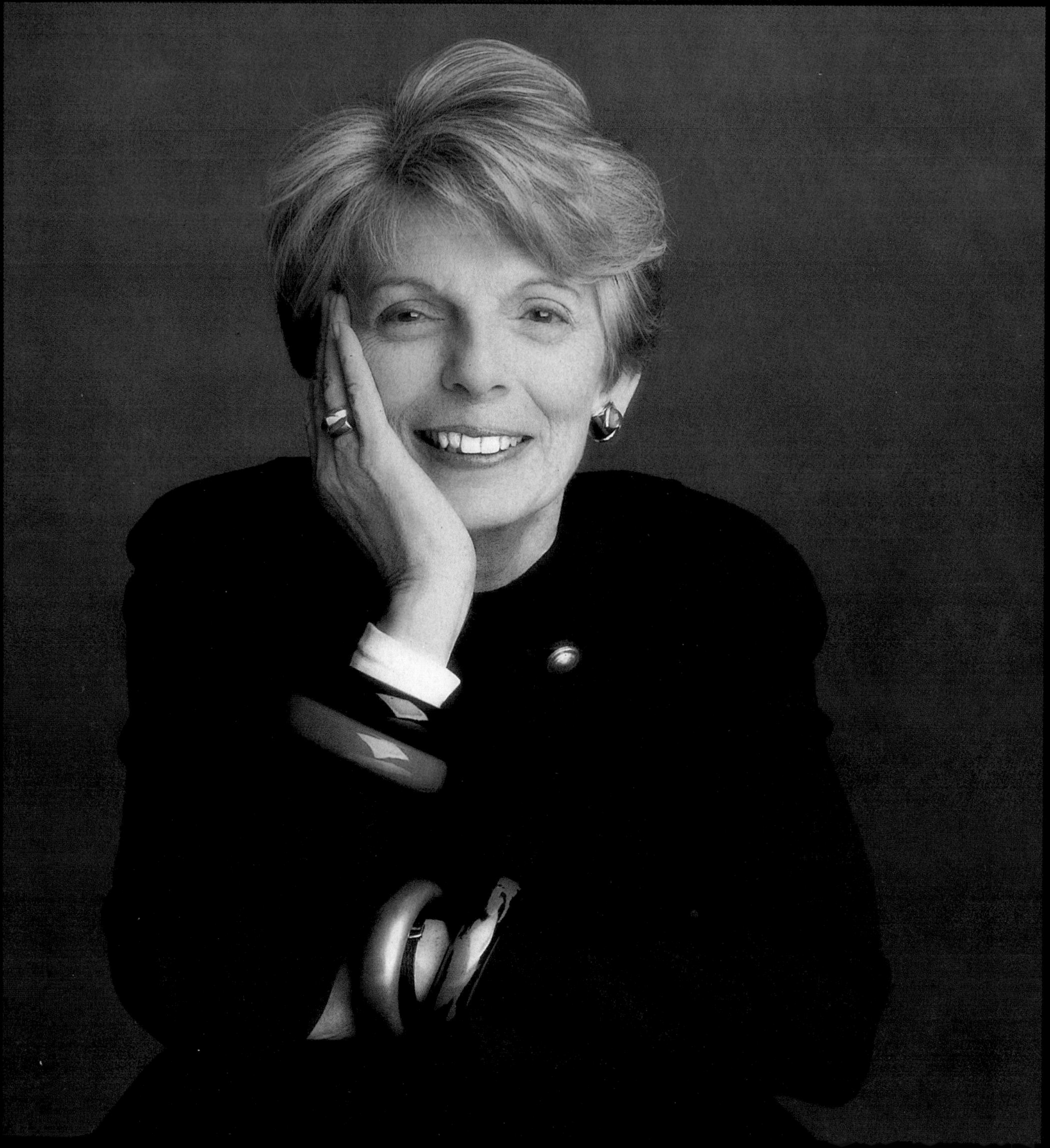

they may not realize that so are Oscar awardees Anne Bancroft, Susan Sarandon, and Anjelica Huston.

Other equally talented Italian-American women work behind the cameras as powerhouses at the highest levels of entertainment. In television, Patricia Fili-Krushel, former president of ABC, became the first woman ever to head a television network. Debra DiMaio received six Emmy Awards between 1986 and 1994, during the eight seasons she produced Oprah Winfrey's popular television talk show. And in 1988, with *Big,* only the second film she had ever directed, Penny Marshall (born Carole Penny Masciarelli) became the first woman ever to direct a film that grossed more than $100 million at the box office.

More recently, two Italian-American business executives were identified by *Fortune* magazine as among the fifty most powerful women in the United States: Patricia Russo, formerly the executive vice president and chief executive officer of service provider networks at Lucent Technologies (and one of the only women at an executive level in the company); and Nina Di Sesa, the chairwoman and chief creative officer of McCann-Erickson, one of the world's largest advertising agencies.

In the competitive market of American publishing, Pamela Fiori and Grace Mirabella have reached the highest levels of authority. Fiori is editor-in-chief and publisher of *Town & Country* magazine, while Mirabella completed her distinguished career as editor of *Vogue* to launch a new magazine named after her: *Mirabella,* which is no longer in circulation.

During the same decade, Rose Marie Bravo became president of Saks Fifth Avenue and now heads Burberry International, while Gabriella Forte is

Left: Grace Mirabella, former editor of *Vogue,* was also editor of *Mirabella,* a magazine named in her honor.

Above: Helen Boehm, chairman of the board of Boehm Enterprises.

in charge of Calvin Klein's vast empire.

Today, Italian-American women have reached positions of great responsibility in this nation. Nevertheless, most of these successful women would agree that their finest achievement has been their ability to balance career and family, thus reconciling their Italian values with the demands of modern life and their own ambition. These daughters and granddaughters of Italian immigrants were trailblazers who broke new ground in business and industry, in government and labor, in sports, science, and entertainment—not only for Italian-American women but for *all* women in the United States. Their mothers were dedicated to running a home. Their daughters might one day be running the country.

Christina Ricci is one of the rare child actors who has successfully managed a transition to serious adult actress.

ITALIAN
AMERICAN
WOMEN

197

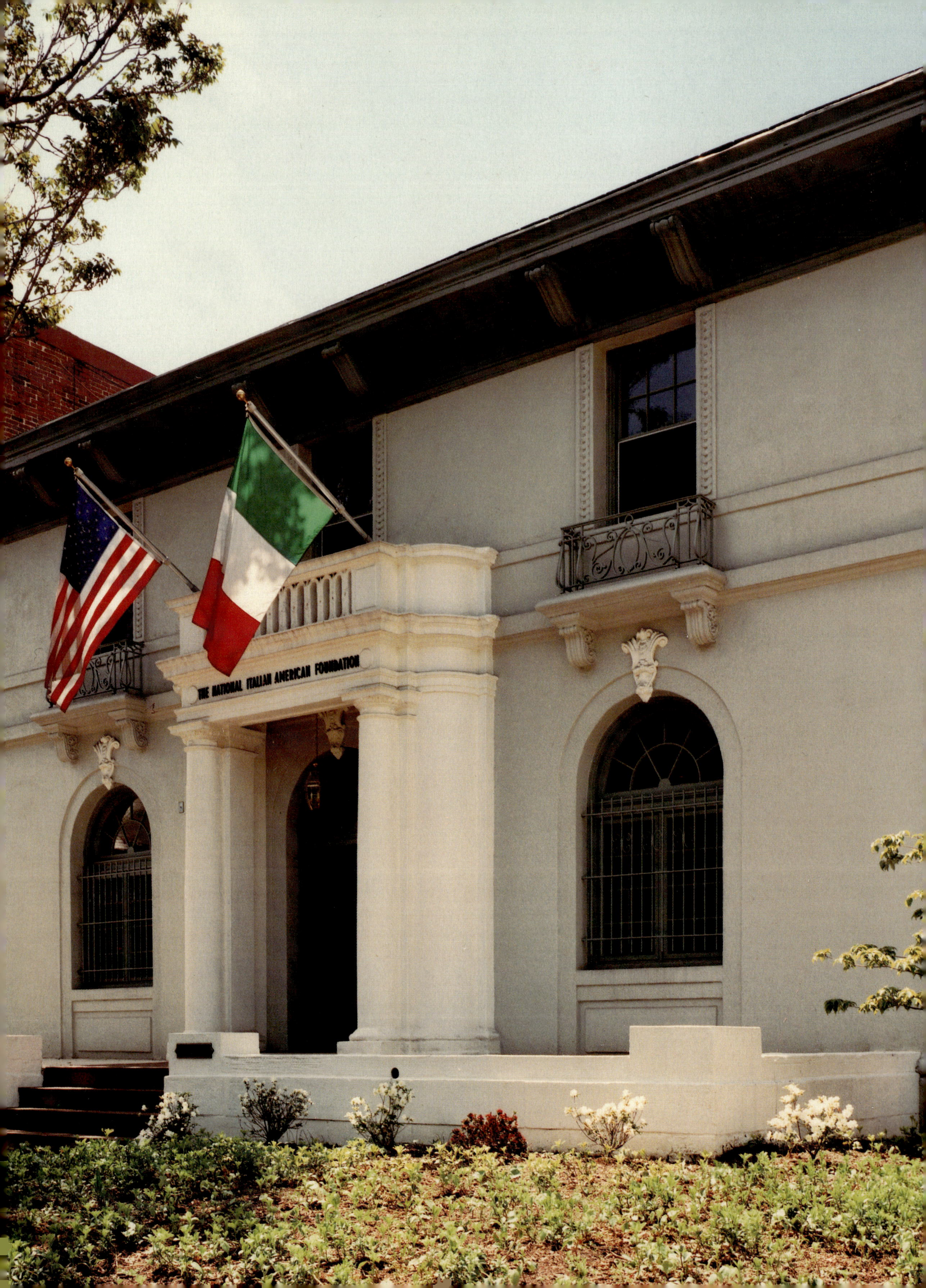
THE NATIONAL ITALIAN AMERICAN FOUNDATION

ITALIAN AMERICANS IN THE MAINSTREAM

At the dawn of the third millennium, Italian Americans are completely integrated into the nation's social and political structures. The most obvious sign of their Americanization is the rapid disappearance of Little Italys.

As we saw in the first three chapters, the estimated five million Italian immigrants who arrived in America between 1880 and 1920 formed neighborhoods that often became true cities within cities. In these communities, Italians tended to band together in an effort to overcome the loneliness and isolation of living in a foreign country. These Little Italys were miniature reproductions of the towns the immigrants had left behind. Almost everyone who lived there was Italian, and spoke various regional dialects. Everything—from diet to religion—was Italian. It was as though a slice of Italy had been brought intact from the other side of the Atlantic Ocean, and the people in the neighborhood tried to keep it alive and defend it from outside influences.

Gradually, Italians began to overcome their feelings of isolation and alienation, becoming energetic participants in the life of the nation, especially through economic, political, and military activities. As their fear of separation from the ethnic community diminished, so did the size and number of the Little Italys. When the world outside was no longer perceived as a threat, Italians were free to move confidently toward Americanization and cultural assimilation.

Today, the Little Italys are much changed. Many are occupied by other new immigrant groups, or have become generic residential areas. In New York,

The National Italian American Foundation headquarters in Washington, D.C.

for instance, home to the largest Italian community in America during the early twentieth century, Little Italy has slowly filled with Asian immigrants who arrived after the 1950s and has been whittled down in size by the neighboring Chinatown.

Today's Italian Americans, descendants of the immigrants who once lived in the Little Italys, have moved out to the suburbs or to middle-class neighborhoods in the city. A University of Chicago study conducted from 1972 to the present has established that the majority of Italian Americans still reside in or near the great cities of the Northeast where they were born. It has also revealed that they earn an average of $32,600 per capita, as compared to a $29,800 national average. This affluency in part explains the tendency of Italian Americans to settle in the wealthier areas of the nation's large cities. Their increasing economic power is directly related to the fact that Italian Americans now hold more prestigious and well-paying jobs. The 1990 census, for example, revealed that two-thirds of Italian Americans in the work force hold white collar jobs.

Education among Italian Americans has also increased significantly. Today they have an average of 12.9 years of schooling as compared to the 12.7 years of non-Italians.

Other statistics from the University of Chicago study give a more complete picture of modern Italian Americans. In politics, for example, there has been a significant switch of loyalty from the Democratic to the Republican party. In the 1970s, 17 percent of Italian Americans declared themselves Republicans and 45 percent Democrats. Today 35 percent of Italian Americans say they are Republicans, 32 percent are Democrats, and the remaining 33 percent, Independent.

This move toward a more conservative political credo notwithstanding, Italian Americans take a liberal stand on many social issues. Most people surveyed said they who would vote for a woman as president of the United States, were "pro-choice" on abortion, and would like the federal government to spend more on health care, education, and the underprivileged.

The same study reveals that there has been an increase in marriages of Italian Americans to those of different ethnic background, so that only about one-third of Italian-Americans surveyed had married a spouse of Italian descent. Italian-American families are still strong. The survey found that 73 percent of

Italian American children live in the same house with both of their parents and nearly half of all Italian-American families—46 percent care for elderly family members at home (a percentage higher than that of other ethnic groups).

The large Italian families of a hundred years ago, each with between five and twelve children, have become a distant memory. Italian-American families, riding on the crest of progress and assimilation, have settled at an average of one to two children per family, about the same as found in other American families.

These statistics demonstrate that the Italian Americans' assimilation into the fabric of American society is complete. This process, however, has had negative repercussions that the new generations of Italian Americans are attempting to remedy. These negative effects include an inability to speak Italian, and an unfortunate ignorance of the history, traditions, and customs of Italy. Nevertheless, seen from a historic perspective, this distancing from their roots can be considered the natural consequence of the process of integration into a foreign culture common to all ethnic groups.

As we have seen in previous chapters, before World War II Italian Americans were forced to deal with hostility and alienation, especially in the years from 1880 to 1940. The children of the original immigrants, born and raised in the United States, experienced a kind of cultural schizophrenia. They were exposed to the American way of life in school but were under strong Italian influence at home. Moreover, many second-generation Italians, identifying their ethnic origins as the cause of the discrimination to which they were subjected, began to reject their roots and sometimes even resented their own parents, perceiving them as ignorant, fatalistic, and backward. On a sociological level, this reaction was, to varying degrees, a denial of their own origins, which were seen as a cause for shame and humiliation. Burying the past in order to step into the future seemed to be the only choice for many second- and third-generation Italian Americans.

The Italian Americans of today, however, with only rare exceptions, no longer feel discriminated against or threatened by their own past. They have entered the mainstream of American society without feelings of inferiority, are confident enough to rediscover the country of their ancestors and to explore its culture, cuisine, and language. They are the bridge between past and future, the link between two civilizations that until less than a century ago seemed incompatible.

Thanks to families such as the Zambellis in Pennsylvania and the Gruccis in New York State, the fireworks market has become yet another source of ethnic pride and profits. These families have provided stunning spectacles for celebrations held at the Statue of Liberty and for the inaugurations of various American presidents since the time of Eisenhower. Italian Americans have proved to be very much like those fireworks: energetic, dynamic, and able to rise sky-high.

The young Italian Americans of today no longer experience the pain of opposing cultural pulls. Nor do they feel obligated to make a choice between the land of their ancestors and the country where they were born. They are comfortable with their American identity yet eager to learn more about the country of their forefathers.

Recent studies show that many young people visit Italy on vacations. Some choose to visit Italy's important cities, learning about art, history, and culinary traditions. Others are making a pilgrimage to the towns of their ancestors, seeking out the places that have been a part of their family's history for generations.

This blossoming genealogical interest is accompanied by an increasing enrollment in Italian-language classes in public and private institutions and in a growing interest in Italian publications available in the United States. Such a process of reconciliation is essential to the survival of Italian Americans' ethnic identity. The validity of the term *Italian American* will be determined by the degree to which people of Italian descent are able to reclaim that part of their cultural patrimony lost during the process of Americanization.

The future of Italian Americans depends, therefore, on their ability to preserve an ethnic individuality. The 1,600-plus Italian-American organizations and institutes that exist throughout the United States are proof of the strong sense of identity and pride Italian Americans today take in their roots.

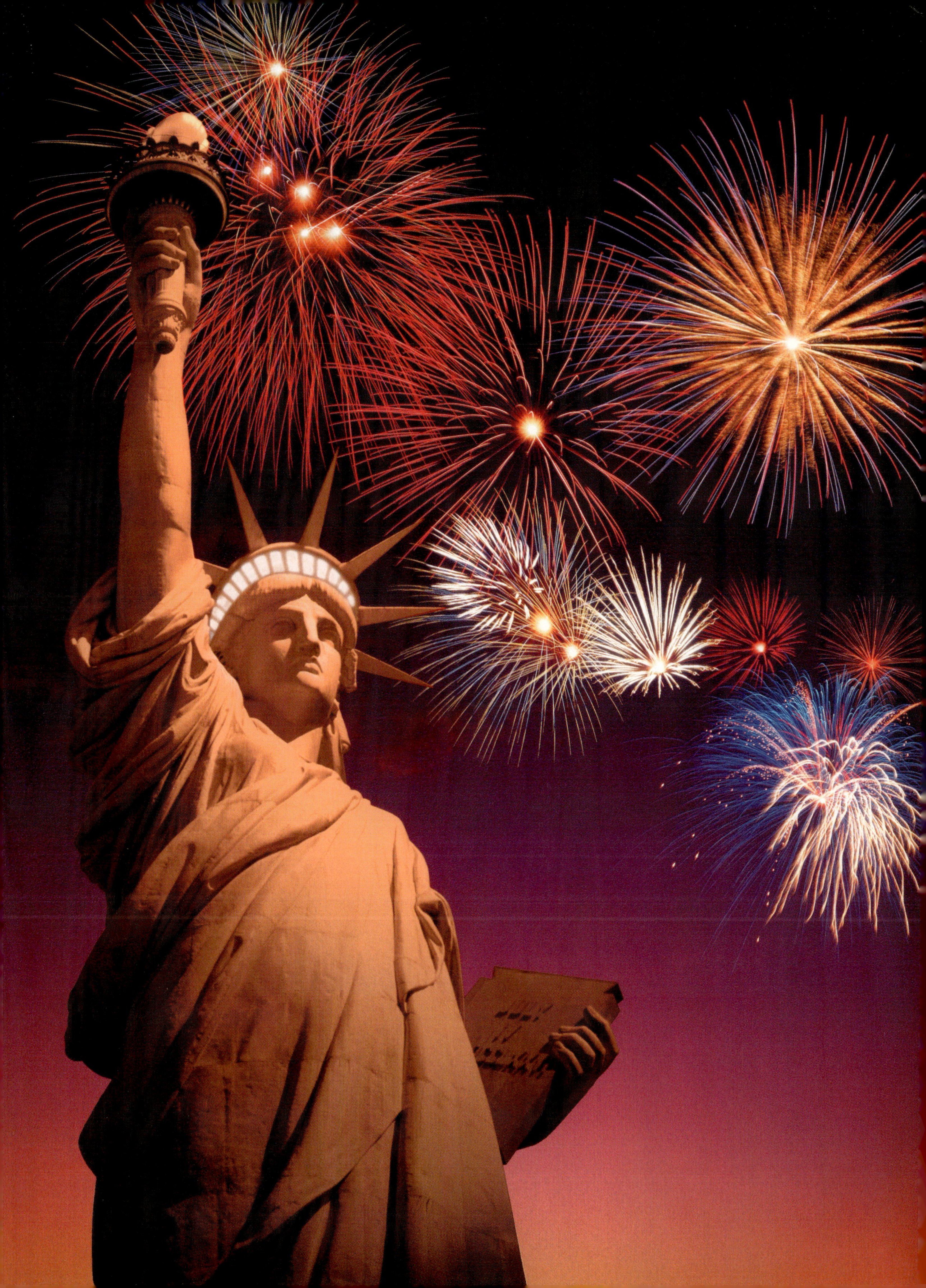

AFTERWORD

Maria Bartiromo of CNBC-TV.

You have just finished reading *Italians in America: A Celebration,* which documents more than two centuries of Italian-American history and culture. Central to that experience is the fact that, when our ancestors came here, the United States thought of itself as a vast melting pot into which each immigrant group contributed its culture and traditions, its customs, language, food, and music.

Most of these immigrants came from Europe, and so it was that throughout the nineteenth century, successive waves of German, Irish, Italian, and Eastern European immigrants gave their new American homeland the best of the Old World's culture while encouraging their children to become American.

How times have changed! Today, at the dawning of a new century, a number of groups with strong ethnic, religious, or racial identities appear to harbor a sense of alienation from the larger American society and a deep distrust of American government and justice. Almost daily the news media report on incidents that indicate cultural and racial wars that have the potential to tear our country apart. The result is that we now have a polarized nation—a nation, as some journalists have put it, of "hyphenated Americans."

Americans are justly concerned about this "Balkanization" of our society. They fear that holding strong ethnic, religious, or racial identities might lead to only a tepid loyalty to America and what it stands for.

Italian Americans, however, as this book so richly illustrates, are the exception. They have successfully balanced their love of Italy and its cultural patrimony with a strong allegiance and deep gratitude to the United States, the country that gave their ancestors opportunities that Italy was unable to offer them. In other words, the enduring appreciation, pride, and respect for the rich heritage they have received from Italy has not prevented Italian Americans from embracing an unwavering loyalty to the United States.

In this sense, Italian Americans are unique among America's many ethnic groups. They alone have succeeded in building a spiritual bridge between their Italian past and their American future. This bridge frees them of a sense of divided loyalties and allows them to love both Italy and the United States as naturally as a child loves both its mother and its father. Go to any meeting of an Italian-American club or organization and there you will find proudly displayed both the American and the Italian flags.

One of their greatest achievements in bicultural adaptation is the ability modern Italian Americans have to preserve the family values that their immigrant forebears brought here more than a century ago. Recent studies of American ethnic groups, including one from the respected University of Chicago, reveal that Italian-American families rank number one for having dinner together regularly. Italian Americans also rank high among those with the most two-parent families, and families that have elderly relatives living with them.

On the other hand, Italian Americans are among those groups with the lowest number of people who are divorced, unemployed, on welfare, or in prison. Social scientists cannot explain the reasons for the stability of Italian-American families, but part of the answer might be found in the clear, uncomplicated values they learned as children. And so, in turn, they teach their children that people are more important than things, that we are our brothers' (*and* sisters', *and* parents') keepers, and that food is a daily celebration of life.

Holding on to Old World values like these while assimilating into modern American society has made Italian Americans a people with two cultures but one heart. As a result, they are admirable role models for other ethnic groups that wish to honor their roots without alienating themselves from America, the land that gave so many an opportunity to develop the best they had to offer.

The National Italian American Foundation preserves and protects these values so that the next generation of Italian Americans, tempered by hard work, disciplined by loving families, and proud of their American and Italian roots, can make their contribution to the United States.

Italians in America: A Celebration documents these achievements and, if past is prologue, portends even greater success in America to the children of Columbus.

MARIA BARTIROMO

Maria Bartiromo reports on American finance for CNBC-TV.

OBERT ALDA · TONY FRANCIOSA · BEN GAZZARA · VIN
RENDA VACCARO · SUSAN SARANDON · ANJELICA HUS
CIORRA · MIRA SORVINO · MADONNA · CHRISTINA RIC
FRANCIS FORD COPPOLA · MICHAEL CIMINO · BRIAN D
TANLEY TUCCI · PENNY MARSHALL · NANCY SAVOCA ·
E VITO · JOE PESCI · NICOLAS CAGE · DANNY AIELLO ·
HAZZ PALMINTERI · VINCENT D'ONOFRIO · LEONARD
ALENTI · JOHN F. ANTIOCO · DOMINICK "NICK" LAROC
ARENTI · JOE VENUTI . BUCKY PIZZARELLI . LOUIS PRIM
RUSS COLOMBO · PERRY COMO · FRANK SINATRA · DEA
IC DAMONE · TONY BENNETT · SONNY BONO · FRANK
TEEN · GIUSEPPE CERACCHI · GIOVANNI ANDREI . GIUS
UIGI PERSICO · GEORGE GIANNETTI · COSTANTINO BRU
RAZIO PICCIRILLI . JOHN RAPETTI · JOSEPH NICOLOSI
ALPH FASANELLA · TOM DISALVO · PASCAL D'ANGELO
I DONATO · JOHN FANTE · JOHN CIARDI · JERRE MANG
PINELLI · ROSA MARIA SEGALE · HELEN BAROLINI · BA
AOLUCCI · RINA FERRARELLI · GAY TALESE · MARGARE
OTHER FRANCES CABRINI · MARIANA BERTOLA · ROSI
LEANOR CUTRI SMEAL · AILEEN RIOTTO SIREY · MARY
IMAIO · PENNY MARSHALL · PATRICIA FILI-KRUSHEL ·
AMILLE PAGLIA · RACHEL GUIDO DE VRIES · LYNN VAN
AZAN · PATRICIA DE STACY HARRISON · JOHN NOBILI
ATHER GIOVANNI GRASSI · FATHER ANTHONY CIAMPI
ALLY SCARAMELLI · ANGELO BARTLETT GIAMATTI · FR
INCENZO BOTTA · CHARLES CONSTANTINE PISE · CAM
OSEMARIE TRUGLIO · ANTONIO MEUCCI · GAETANO L
NRICO FERMI · ALFONSO TAMMARO · JOSEPH T. GEMM
ICCARDO GIACCONI · BRUNO ROSSI · FRANK PAOLINI
URIA · GIULIO NATTA · LOUIS IGNARRO · RITA LEVI-MO
NTONIO IACORIO · VINCENT CICCONE · EDMUND P